ROMANTASY CROCHET CLUB

20 Epic Projects
for Your Reading
Journeys

AMANDA SENNETT

CONTENTS

3 Wear the Fantasy 67

4 Fantastical Creatures & Amazing Animals 81

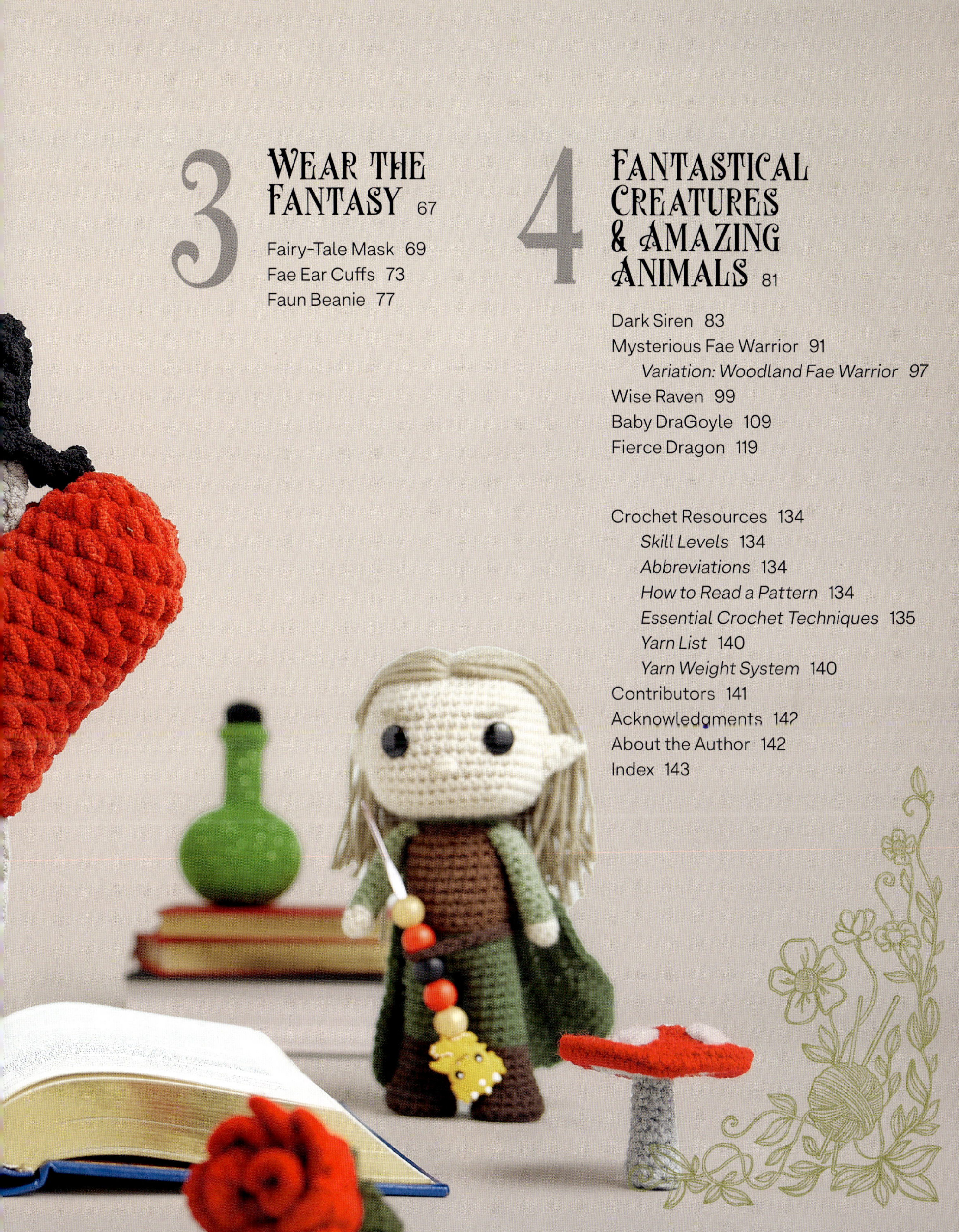

INTRODUCTION

Dear fellow bookish crocheter,

Do you ever find yourself wishing you could wrap your love for romantasy *around* you like a cozy blanket? Whether you're dreaming of star-crossed lovers or of epic quests in far-off lands, it feels like we book lovers have been *starved* for the perfect merch that bring our favorite stories to life. I know the feeling—I've searched high and low for magical book-inspired decor and accessories, only to come up short. So, when Joy Aquilino at Quarry Books/Quarto Publishing Group approached me with the idea of creating a crochet book inspired by the romantasy genre, I couldn't say no!

Within these enchanted pages, you'll discover more than 20 delightful patterns that allow you to wear your love for romantasy on your sleeve! Whether it's for your bookshelves, your walls, or your wardrobe, these projects are a way to bring a bit of your favorite fictional worlds into your own.

As a diehard sci-fi and fantasy fan, I squealed when the opportunity to put together this project landed in my lap. Like so many of you, I've been obsessed with fantasy since I was young. Once I discovered romantasy, there was no turning back. My journey began with a reading challenge at my local library in 2022, and it only took one audiobook—Sarah J. Maas's *A Court of Thorns and Roses*—to send me tumbling headlong into the rabbit hole of fae courts, cursed princes, and starry-eyed heroines. (Let's be honest, this series hooked all of us!)

Since then, my to-be-read list has become an epic quest of its own, filled with more than 100 books—nearly all romantasy! Some of my favorites are Maas's *Throne of Glass* series, *The Cruel Prince* by Holly Black, *Fourth Wing* by Rebecca Yarros, *One Dark Window* by Rachel Gillig, and *Shatter Me* by Tahereh Mafi. And the list keeps growing, as I'm sure your TBR (To Be Read) pile does!

Pairing my love of these fantastical worlds with the meditative magic of crochet has been an absolute dream. There's something deeply satisfying about listening to an audiobook while my hands work their own bit of crafting magic. It's the perfect escape, and I hope you'll feel the same way as you crochet the projects in this book.

About the QR Codes
The QR codes throughout this book offer access to short video tutorials that clarify or demonstrate some of the techniques that are used to create the projects. Just scan each code with your smartphone's camera to view a quick lesson!

This journey was made even more special by the fellowship of the incredibly talented crochet designers who joined me. We laughed, created, and let our imaginations soar, just like the heroines and heroes of the books we love. The seven designers who contributed to this book are each beyond brilliant, and I'm thrilled to introduce them to you:

- Staci Burns of Fiddlesticks Crochet
- Lara Carter of Hookedonewe_x
- Jodie Chadwick of Handmade by Jodie
- Sonia Childers of S.Crochet.Designs
- Daniella Flete of Daniella's Workshop
- Mary Penney of Little Brute Creations
- Jessica Ryan of Eclectic Jess

So, grab your hooks, cue up your favorite audiobook, and prepare to embark on a creative journey filled with romance, adventure, and a dash of magic. I hope each project feels like stepping into a new fantastical world—one stitch at a time.

Happy crocheting, and may your yarn be ever enchanted!
—Amanda

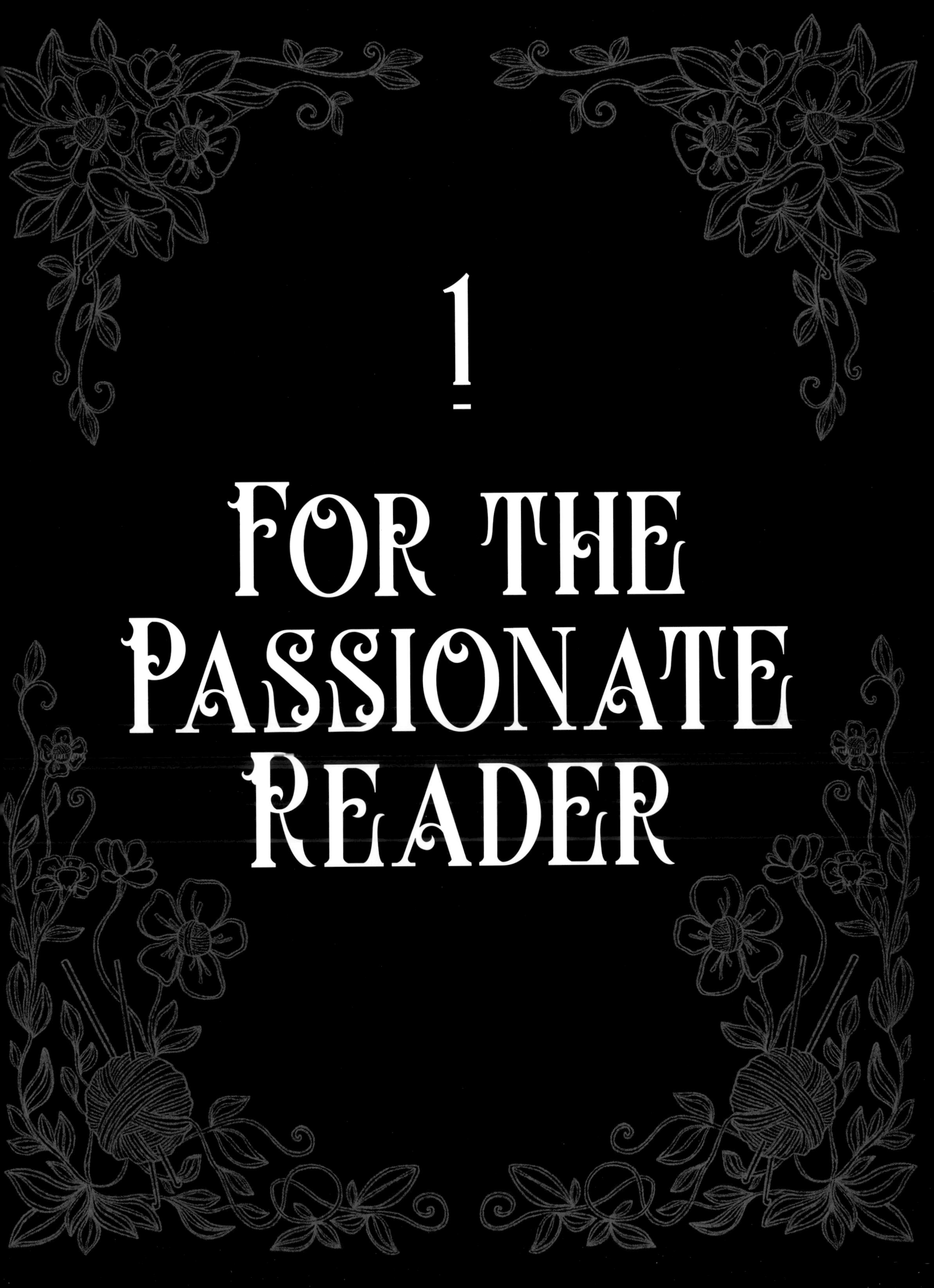

1

For the Passionate Reader

Book Lover's Bookmark Trio

Designed by Amanda Sennett of Crochet By A Manda Lorian

The point of view just switched to the mysterious Shadow Daddy, but the clock has struck 2 a.m. and it's a work night. Time to mark your page with the heavenly touch of an **Angel's Wing** or the seductive swish of a **Dragon's Tail**. If your 900-page epic needs something with a bigger (ahem) wingspan, might we recommend a perfect pair of **Bat Wings** to make sure you never lose your place?

Skill Level

Measurements

- Bat Wings made with sport weight yarn (#3 light) and recommended hook size: measures approx. 9¼" (23.5 cm) long.
- Dragon's Tail made with sport weight yarn (#3 light) and recommended hook size: measures approx. 7¾" (19.7 cm) long.
- Angel's Wing made with sport weight yarn (#3 light) and recommended hook size: measures approx. 15" (38.1 cm) long; wing only: 5¼" (13.3 cm) long.

Yarn

- Sport weight yarn (#3 light) in black (for Bat Wings bookmark), white (for Angel Wing bookmark), and dragon body and dragon tail accent colors of your choice (for Dragon Tail bookmark).
- *Shown:* Sport Weight I Love This Yarn (2½ oz/70 g, 230 yd/210 m, 100% acrylic) in Black (30), White (10), and Green (185)
- Less than 1 skein of each color is required.

Crochet Hook

- 2.75 mm (size C/2). *Note:* This is my preferred hook size, but you may need to use a different size if you are prone to loose or tight tension.

Notions

Scissors
Tapestry needle

Gauge

Gauge is not critical for these projects.

Notes

- Instructions are provided for three different bookmarks: Bat Wings, Dragon's Tail, and Angel's Wing.
- Each bookmark is made in pieces that are sewn together to complete the bookmark.
- It is possible that the bookmarks could curl at the edges. To fix the curling, either press the bookmark inside a heavy book for a couple of days or gently press with an iron. If using an iron, be sure to use low heat and place a towel between the bookmark and the iron to prevent scorching the yarn.

BAT WINGS (MAKE 2)

With black yarn, leaving a long beginning tail for sewing, ch 5.

Row 1: Sc in 2nd ch from hook and in next 3 ch, turn—4 sts.

Row 2: Ch 1, sc in each st across, turn.

Row 3: Ch 1, 2 sc in first st, sc in each st across, turn—5 sts.

Row 4: Ch 1, 2 sc in first st, sc in each st to last st, 2 sc in last st, turn—7 sts.

Rows 5 and 6: Rep Rows 3 and 4—10 sts in Row 6.

Row 7: Ch 1, sc in each st across, turn.

Row 8: Ch 2, sc in 2nd ch from hook, sc in each st to last st, 2 sc in last st, turn—12 sts.

Row 9: Ch 3, sc in 3rd ch from hook, sc in next 11 sts; leave last st unworked, turn—12 sts.

Row 10: Ch 1, 2 sc in first st, sc in next 9 sts; leave last 2 sts unworked, turn—11 sts.

Row 11: Ch 1, sc in each st to last st, 2 sc in last st, turn—12 sts.

Rows 12–14: Ch 1, 2 sc in first st, sc in each st to last st, 2 sc in last st, turn—18 sts in Row 14.

Row 15: Ch 3, sc in 3rd ch from hook, sc in each st across, turn—19 sts.

Row 16: Ch 2, sc in 2nd ch from hook, sc in next 18 sts; leave last st unworked, turn—19 sts.

Row 17: Do not ch, sk first st, sc2tog, sc in next 15 sts; leave last st unworked, turn—16 sts.

Row 18: Do not ch, sk first st, sc in next 13 sts, sc2tog, turn—14 sts.

Row 19: Do not ch, sk first st, sc2tog, sc in next 9 sts, sc2tog, turn—11 sts.

Row 20: Ch 1, 2 sc in first st, sc in each st to last 2 sts, sc2tog, turn.

Row 21: Do not ch, sk first st, sc2tog, sc in each st to last st, 2 sc in last st, turn—10 sts.

Rows 22–25: Rep Rows 20 and 21 twice—8 sts in Row 25.

Row 26: Ch 3, sc in 3rd ch from hook, sl st in next st; leave remaining sts unworked.

Fasten off.

With beginning tails, sew the two wings together in the center.

Fasten off and weave in ends.

DRAGON'S TAIL

With dragon body color, ch 9.

Row 1: Sc in 2nd ch from hook and in each ch across, turn—8 sts.

Rows 2–4: Ch 1, sc in each st across, turn.

Row 5: Ch 1, sc in next 3 sts, sc2tog, sc in next 3 sts, turn—7 sts.

Rows 6–9: Ch 1, sc in each st across, turn (4 rows).

Row 10: Ch 1, sc in next 2 sts, sc2tog, sc in next 3 sts, turn—6 sts.

Rows 11–15: Ch 1, sc in each st across, turn (5 rows).

Row 16: Ch 1, sc in next 2 sts, sc2tog, sc in next 2 sts, turn—5 sts.

Rows 17–21: Ch 1, sc in each st across, turn (5 rows).

Row 22: Ch 1, sc in next 2 sts, sc2tog, sc in next st, turn—4 sts.

Rows 23–27: Ch 1, sc in each st across, turn (5 rows).

Row 28: Ch 1, sc in next st, sc2tog, sc in next st, turn—3 sts.

Rows 29–33: Ch 1, sc in each st across, turn (5 rows).

Row 34: Ch 1, sc2tog, sc in next st, turn—2 sts.

Rows 35–39: Ch 1, sc in each st across, turn (5 rows).

Row 40: Ch 1, sc2tog, turn—1 st.

Rows 41 and 42: Ch 1, sc in next st, turn (2 rows).

Row 43: Ch 1, sl st in next st.

Fasten off.

Tail Fins (make 2)

With dragon tail accent color, ch 9.

Row 1: Sc in 2nd ch from hook and in next 6 ch, 2 sc in last ch, turn—9 sts.

Row 2: Working in BLO, 2 sc in next st, sc in next 6 sts, sc2tog, turn.

Row 3: Do not ch, sk first st; working in BLO, sc in next 7 sts, 2 sc in last st, turn.

Rows 4 and 5: Rep Rows 2 and 3.

Fasten off, leaving a long tail for sewing.

Sew tail fins to each side of the pointed end of the dragon tail.

Weave in ends.

ANGEL'S WING

Special Stitch

- **htr:** Yarn over two times, insert hook into stitch, pull up a loop, yarn over and pull through two loops, yarn over and pull through the three remaining loops.

Note: This piece is worked in the BLO (back loops only) unless working in a chain or it is otherwise impossible.

With white yarn, make a magic ring.

Row 1: Work 4 sc into ring, turn.

Row 2: Ch 1, 2 sc in each st across, turn—8 sts.

Row 3: Ch 1, sc in each st across, turn.

Row 4: Ch 1, [sc in next st, 2 sc in next st] 4 times, turn—12 sts.

Row 5: Ch 1, sc in each st across, turn.

Row 6: Ch 1, [sc in next 2 sts, 2 sc in next st] 2 times, hdc in next 2 sts, 2 dc in next st, dc in next st, htr in next st, 2 tr in last st, do not turn—16 sts.

Row 7: Ch 1, working in ends of rows, work 17 sc evenly spaced along straight lower edge, turn.

Row 8: Ch 4, sc in 2nd ch from hook and in next 2 ch, sl st in first st of Row 7; leave remaining sts unworked, turn—3 sts (not including the sl st).

Row 9: Ch 1, sk sl st, sc in each st across, turn.

Row 10: Ch 3, sc in 2nd ch from hook and in next ch, sc in each st across, sl st in next unworked st of Row 7, turn—5 sts (not including the sl st).

Row 11: Ch 1, sk sl st, sc in each st to last st; leave last st unworked, turn—4 sts.

Row 12: Ch 2, sc in 2nd ch from hook, sc in each st across, sl st in next unworked st of Row 7, turn—5 sts (not including the sl st).

Row 13: Ch 1, sk sl st, sc in each st to last st; leave last st unworked, turn—4 sts.

Rows 14–29: Rep Rows 10–13 four more times—8 sts in Row 29.

Rows 30–39: Rep Rows 10 and 11 five more times—13 sts in Row 39.

Row 40: Rep Row 10—15 sts (not including the sl st).

Fasten off and weave in tail.

Attach yarn at the end of Row 7 (the smaller end of the wing).

Ch 51 (or to desired length). Turn, sc in 2nd ch from hook and in each ch across.

Fasten off and weave in ends.

Werewolf Tablet or Book Sleeve

Designed by Lara Carter of Hookedonewe_x

You've stuffed your tablet to the brim with pure literary goodness, but danger lurks around every corner, red in tooth and claw. Keep your e-reader safe from the fierce grip of the wild (and the peering eyes of those around you) with this werewolf-inspired sleeve. The only thing more primal than its hold on your book? The unbreakable bond between fated mates!

Skill Level

Measurements

- Sleeve made with bulky weight yarn (#5 bulky) or super bulky weight yarn (#6 super bulky) and recommended hook size: measures approx. 9" (23 cm) tall.

Yarn

- Super bulky weight yarn (#6 super bulky) in black and black fur
- Bulky weight yarn (#5 bulky) in gray, white, and white fur
- *Shown:* Yarn Bee Cozy Occasion (5.5 oz/156 g, 101 yd/92.4 m, 100% polyester) in Black (36)
- Yarn Bee Fur the Moment (3.5 oz/100 g, 62 yd/57 m, 100% polyester) in Black (30)
- Less than 1 skein of each color is required.

Crochet Hook

- 4 mm (size G/6). *Note:* This is my preferred hook size, but you may need to use a different size if you are prone to loose or tight tension.

Materials

20 mm flat back safety eyes
Flat back safety nose (optional)
Fabric glue or hot glue

Notions

Scissors
Stitch markers
Tapestry needle

Gauge

Gauge is not critical for this project.

Note

- This is made with the 6.8" (17.5 cm) Kindle Paperwhite in mind. Modification instructions are simple: just shorten the original starting chain or add more rows to the pattern to change height or width.

BODY

With gray yarn, ch 30.

Rnd 1: Sc in 2nd ch from hook and in next 27 ch, 4 sc in last ch; working along opposite side of foundation ch, sc in next 28 ch, 3 sc in next ch—62 sts.

Place a marker in last st made to indicate end of rnd. Move marker up as each rnd is completed.

Rnd 2: Sc in each st around.

Rnds 3–10: Hdc in each st around (8 rnds).

Change to white yarn.

Rnds 11 and 12: Working in BLO, hdc in each st around (2 rnds).

Change to gray yarn.

Rnds 13–16: Hdc in each st around (4 rnds).

Rnd 17: [Sc in next st, sc2tog] 20 times, sc in last 2 sts—42 sts.

Rnd 18: Sc in each st around.

Depending on your tension, you may not be at the side of the sleeve; sc around until you are.

Fasten off and weave in ends.

EARS (MAKE 2)

With white yarn, ch 5.

Row 1: Sc in 2nd ch from hook and in next 3 ch, turn—4 sts.

Row 2: Ch 1, [sc2tog] 2 times, turn—2 sts.

Row 3: Ch 1, sc in next 2 sts, turn.

Row 4: Ch 1, sc2tog, turn—1 st.

Row 5: Ch 1, sc in st.

Change to gray yarn.

Row 6: Sc evenly spaced all the way around outer edge of ear, working 2 sc in each corner.

Fasten off, leaving a long tail for sewing.

ASSEMBLY

1. Sew ears to sleeve, leaving 2 sts between edge of each ear and side edge of sleeve.
2. Attach eyes to sleeve, beneath the inside edge of each ear between Rnds 15 and 16.
3. Attach nose centered one round beneath eyes. Instead of using a flat safety nose, the nose can be embroidered with a long strand of black yarn.

FUR STRIPE

Draw up a loop of white fur yarn in first free front loop from Rnd 11, ch 1, hdc in same loop and in each free front loop from Rnds 11 and 12.

Fasten off and weave in ends.

VARIATION

WOLF

Yarn Shown:

Loops & Threads Sweet Snuggles Lite (8.8 oz/250 g, 218 yd/200 m, 100% polyester) in Gray and White

Yarn Bee Fur the Moment (3.5 oz/100 g, 62 yd/57 m, 100% polyester) in Cream (1)

Less than 1 skein of each color is required for each piece.

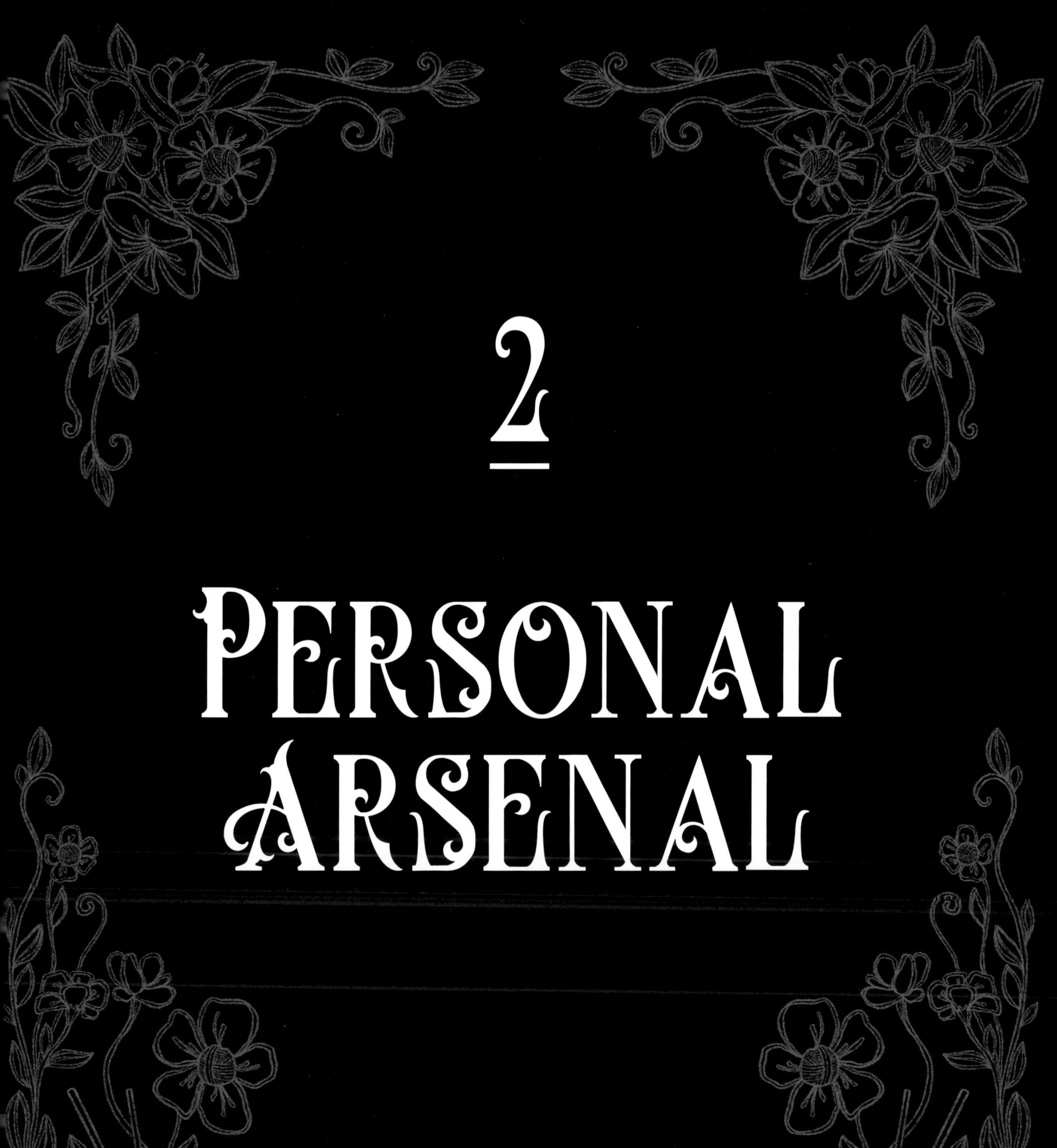

2

Personal Arsenal

Poisoned Apples

Designed by Amanda Sennett of Crochet By A Manda Lorian

Every wicked queen knows her way around a poisoned apple. Whether you're dabbling in morally gray areas or plotting your next chess move, these crocheted apples are a juicy addition to your home décor. They won't put anyone to sleep, but they might stop hearts!

Skill Level

Measurements

- Smaller apple made with worsted weight yarn (#4 medium): measures approx. 2 x 2" (5 x 5 cm).
- Larger apple made with super bulky yarn (#6 super bulky): measures approx. 4 x 4" (10 x 10 cm).

Yarn

- Any weight yarn in apple, poison, and stem colors of your choice.
- *Shown:* I Love This Yarn (7 oz/198 g, 355 yd/324 m, 100% acrylic) in Limelight (788), Cinnamon (72), and Black (30)
- Bernat Blanket Yarn (10.5 oz/300 g, 220 yd/201 m, 100% polyester) in Hot Pink Sparkle, Coal, and Taupe
- Less than 1 skein of each color is required.

Crochet Hook

- 2.75 mm (size C/2) crochet hook for worsted weight yarn
- 6 mm (size J/10) crochet hook for super bulky yarn
- *Note:* These are my preferred hook sizes, but you may need to use different sizes if you are prone to loose or tight tension.

Materials

Stuffing

Notions

Scissors
Stitch markers
Tapestry needle

Gauge

Gauge is not critical for this project.

Note

- Do not mix yarn weights. Use the same yarn weight for all three yarn colors.

APPLE

With apple color yarn, make a magic ring.

Rnd 1: Work 6 sc into ring; do not join, work in continuous rnds (spiral).

Place a marker in last st made to indicate end of rnd. Move marker up as each rnd is completed.

Rnd 2: 2 sc in each of next 6 sts—12 sts.

Rnd 3: [Sc in next st, 2 sc in next st] 6 times—18 sts.

Rnd 4: [Sc in next 2 sts, 2 sc in next st] 6 times—24 sts.

Rnd 5: [Sc in next 3 sts, 2 sc in next st] 6 times—30 sts.

Rnds 6–8: Sc in each st around (3 rnds).

Rnd 9: Sc in next 4 sts, sc2tog, [sc in next 8 sts, sc2tog] 2 times, sc in last 4 sts—27 sts.

Rnd 10: [Sc in next 7 sts, sc2tog] 3 times—24 sts.

Rnd 11: Sc in next 3 sts, sc2tog, [sc in next 6 sts, sc2tog] 2 times, sc in last 3 sts—21 sts.

Rnd 12: Sc in each st around.

Stuff the apple firmly. If needed, add more stuffing as you work the next 2 rnds, but be careful not to overstuff.

Rnd 13: [Sc in next st, sc2tog] 7 times—14 sts.

Rnd 14: [Sc2tog] 7 times—7 sts.

Fasten off, leaving a long tail for sewing and shaping. Sew hole closed.

POISON DRIPS

With poison color yarn, make a magic ring.

Rnd 1: Work 7 sc into ring; do not join, work in continuous rnds (spiral).

Place a marker in last st made to indicate end of rnd. Move marker up as each rnd is completed.

Rnd 2: 2 sc in each of next 7 sts—14 sts.

Rnd 3: [Sc in next st, 2 sc in next st] 7 times—21 sts.

Rnd 4: [Sc in next 2 sts, 2 sc in next st] 7 times—28 sts.

Rnd 5: [Sc in next 3 sts, 2 sc in next st] 7 times—35 sts.

Rnds 6 and 7: Sc in each st around (2 rnds).

Rnd 8: [Sl st in next st, sc in next st, hdc in next st, dc in next st, hdc in next st, sc in next st, sl st in next st] 5 times.

Rnd 9: [Sc in next 4 sts, ch 4, hdc in 2nd ch from hook, sl st in each of next 2 ch, sc in next 3 sts] 5 times.

Fasten off, leaving a long tail for sewing.

STEM

With stem color yarn, make a magic ring.

Rnd 1: Work 4 sc into ring; do not join, work in continuous rnds (spiral).

Place a marker in last st made to indicate end of rnd. Move marker up as each rnd is completed.

Rnd 2: Working in BLO, sc in each st around.

Rnd 3: Sc in each st around.

Fasten off, leaving a long tail for sewing.

ASSEMBLY

1. Fit poison drips over the apple, and with the tail from the drips, sew through a stitch at the bottom of each drip to keep in place. Hide tail inside the apple.
2. With the tail from the apple, create the apple shape. Pass the tail up from the bottom of the apple and out the top center (this will also be through the poison drip). Reinsert the needle in a different stitch in the top of the apple, and pass it back down through the bottom. Pull tight and repeat as many times as you like to achieve the proper shape of the apple. Fasten the yarn with a knot, and hide the tail inside the apple.
3. With the tail from the stem, sew the stem into the indentation created at the top of the apple. Tie a knot, and hide the tail inside the apple.

Morally Gray Heart Garland/Wall Hanging

Designed by Jessica Ryan of Eclectic Jess

Not all heroes wear a shining crown—sometimes they wield a dark, seductive power. Hang this morally gray masterpiece as a tribute to your favorite antiheroes. A perfect reminder of the love interests who straddle the line between saving the world and destroying it. When the wind catches it just right, you can almost hear it whisper in a deadly, low voice, *"Who hurt you?"*

Skill Level

Measurements

- One heart made with worsted weight yarn (#4 medium): measures approx. 2¼" (5.5 cm) tall x 2¼" (5.5 cm) wide (at widest).
- A garland made with worsted weight yarn (#4 medium): measures approx. 2¼" (5.5 cm) for the top heart plus 4½" long (11.5 cm) for each additional heart.
- Garland length examples:

Number of Hearts in Garland	*Approx. Length*
4	15¾" (40 cm)
5	20¼" (51.5 cm)
6	24¾" (63 cm)
7	29¼" (74.5 cm)
8	33¾" (85.5 cm)
9	38¼" (97 cm)
10	42¾" (108.5 cm)

Yarn

- Worsted weight yarn (#4 medium) in black, dark gray, medium gray, light gray, and white.
- *Shown:* I Love This Yarn (7 oz/198 g, 355 yd/324 m, 100% acrylic) in Black (30), Light Gray (190), Gray Mist (200), Grey Beard (201), and White (10)
- Less than 1 skein of each color is required.

Crochet Hook

- 4.25 mm (size G). *Note:* This is my preferred hook size, but you may need to use a different size if you are prone to loose or tight tension.

Materials

Café-style curtain rod or wooden dowel, measured to fit your space (referred to as the "rod" throughout the pattern)

Notions

Scissors
Stitch markers
Tapestry needle

Gauge

Gauge is not critical for this project.

Special Stitch

- **htr:** Yarn over two times, insert hook into stitch, pull up a loop, yarn over and pull through two loops, yarn over and pull through the three remaining loops.

Notes

- Any number of garlands can be made and attached to the rod, with any number of hearts in each garland.
- To create an arch effect as shown in photograph, work the two outermost garlands (one for each side edge) using the darkest yarn color with as many hearts as desired. Change to the next lighter color and work the next two garlands (one to hang to the inside of each outermost garland) with one fewer heart. Continue in this manner, working each pair of garlands with the next lighter yarn color and one fewer heart, until a pair of garlands has been worked with each yarn color.

TOP HEART

Hanging Loop Chain

Measure the circumference of the rod.

With yarn color of your choice, make a chain to match the rod circumference plus 2 more chains.

Rnd 1: Work 6 dc in 3rd ch from hook, skip over the hanging loop chain, work 6 more dc in the same (3rd) ch; join with sl st in first dc—12 sts.

Rnd 2:

First Half of Rnd 2: Ch 3 (does not count as a st), (dc, hdc) in same st as joining sl st, 2 sc in each of next 2 sts, (hdc, dc, htr) in next st, 3 tr in next st, dc in next st, ch 1, insert hook in same st as last dc then into the first ch (free end) of the hanging loop chain, yarn over and draw through all loops on hook (forming the hanging chain into a loop); leave remaining sts of Rnd 1 unworked for now—13 sts in this half of Rnd 2.

Note: This completes the first half of the heart, as well as forming the hanging loop. The hanging loop needs to fit around the rod with minimal slack while still being able to move along the rod to the desired position. Test the loop on the rod to ensure it fits well before continuing.

Second Half of Rnd 2: Continuing around, working into the remaining sts of Rnd 1, ch 1, dc in next st, 3 tr in next st, (htr, dc, hdc) in next st, 2 sc in each of next 2 sts, (hdc, dc) in next st; join with sl st in first dc (of first half of Rnd 2)—13 sts in this half of Rnd 2, for a total of 26 sts in Rnd 2.

Do not fasten off.

NEXT HEART

Ch 16. Place a marker in the 6th ch from the hook (you will work into this marked ch in Rnd 2).

Rnd 1: Work 6 dc in 3rd ch from hook, skip over the hanging loop chain, work 6 more dc in the same (3rd) ch; join with sl st in first dc—12 sts.

Rnd 2: Ch 3 (does not count as a st), (dc, hdc) in same st as joining sl st, 2 sc in each of next 2 sts, (hdc, dc, htr) in next st, 3 tr in next st, dc in next st, ch 1, insert hook in same st as last dc then in marked ch of beg ch-16 (remove marker), yarn over and draw through all loops on hook (securing heart to hanging chain), ch 1, dc in next st, 3 tr in next st, (htr, dc, hdc) in next st, 2 sc in each of next 2 sts, (hdc, dc) in next st; join with sl st in first dc—26 sts.

Repeat this Next Heart section until you have the desired number of hearts on your garland.

When your garland is the desired length, fasten off and weave in ends.

Slide the hanging loop from the back of the Top Heart onto your rod.

Scan to watch a video tutorial showing how to make the two types of hearts.

Potion Bottles

Designed by Mary Penney of Little Brute Creations

Whether you're crafting a love potion or keeping a bottle of poison just in case things go wrong, these crocheted potion bottles are the ultimate in romantic alchemy. Be careful with the dosage—too much and your enemies-to-lovers storyline might never get off the ground!

Skill Level

Measurements

- Bottle made with worsted weight yarn (#4 medium): measures approx. 4–6" (10–15 cm) tall.

Yarn

- Any weight yarn in pink, green, and black
- *Shown:* I Love This Yarn (7 oz/198 g, 355 yd/324 m, 100% acrylic) in Mixed Berry (294) and Black (30)
- Big Twist Twinkle (6 oz/170 g, 380 yd/347 m, 97% acrylic, 3% polyester) in Teal
- Less than 1 skein of each color is required.

Crochet Hook

- 2.75 mm (size C/2). *Note:* This is my preferred hook size, but you may need to use a different size if you are prone to loose or tight tension.

Materials

Stuffing

Notions

Scissors
Stitch markers
Tapestry needle

Gauge

Gauge is not critical for this project.

POISON POTION

Bottle

With green yarn, make a magic ring.

Rnd 1: Work 6 sc into ring; do not join, work in continuous rnds (spiral).

Place a marker in last st made to indicate end of rnd. Move marker up as each rnd is completed.

Rnd 2: 2 sc in each of next 6 sts—12 sts.

Rnd 3: [Sc in next st, 2 sc in next st] 6 times—18 sts.

Rnd 4: [Sc in next 2 sts, 2 sc in next st] 6 times—24 sts.

Rnd 5: [Sc in next 3 sts, 2 sc in next st] 6 times—30 sts.

Rnd 6: Working in BLO, sc in each st around.

Rnd 7: [Sc in next 2 sts, 2 sc in next st] 10 times—40 sts.

Rnd 8: Sc in each st around.

Rnd 9: [Sc in next 19 sts, 2 sc in next st] 2 times—42 sts.

Stabilize Bottle (optional): Cut a circle out of cardboard and secure it inside the bottom of the bottle using a small amount of glue. This will help the bottle sit flat.

Rnd 10: [Sc in next 6 sts, 2 sc in next st] 6 times—48 sts.

Rnds 11–14: Sc in each st around (4 rnds).

Rnd 15: [Sc in next 2 sts, sc2tog] 12 times—36 sts.

Rnd 16: [Sc in next st, sc2tog] 12 times—24 sts.

Begin stuffing bottle, and continue to stuff until piece is complete.

Rnd 17: [Sc in next 2 sts, sc2tog] 6 times—18 sts.

Rnd 18: [Sc in next st, sc2tog] 6 times—12 sts.

Rnd 19: Working in FLO, sc in each st around.

Rnds 20–26: Sc in each st around (7 rnds).

Rnd 27: Working in FLO, [sc in next st, 2 sc in next st] 6 times—18 sts.

Rnd 28: Sc in each st around.

Fasten off and weave in ends.

Stopper

With black yarn, make a magic ring.

Rnd 1: Work 6 sc into ring; do not join, work in continuous rnds (spiral).

Place a marker in last st made to indicate end of rnd. Move marker up as each rnd is completed.

Rnd 2: 2 sc in each of next 6 sts—12 sts.

Rnd 3: Working in BLO, sc in each st around.

Rnds 4 and 5: Sc in each st around (2 rnds).

Fasten off, leaving a long tail for sewing.

Stuff the stopper and sew it to the bottle opening using the free back loops from Rnd 19. Tie off and hide the end. *Tip:* Roll the opening down to give you full access to those free back loops.

HEART-SHAPED LOVE POTION

Potion Bottle

Heart Lobes (make 2)

With pink yarn, make a magic ring.

Rnd 1: Work 6 sc into ring; do not join, work in continuous rnds (spiral).

Place a marker in last st made to indicate end of rnd. Move marker up as each rnd is completed.

Rnd 2: 2 sc in each of next 6 sts—12 sts.

Rnd 3: [Sc in next st, 2 sc in next st] 6 times—18 sts.

Rnds 4 and 5: Sc in each st around (2 rnds).

Fasten off first lobe and weave in ends.

Do not fasten off second lobe.

Join Lobes

Rnd 6: Sc in next 16 sts of second lobe; leave last 2 sts of second lobe unworked; beginning anywhere on first lobe, sc in next 16 sts of first lobe; leave last 2 sts of first lobe unworked—32 sts. Work first st of next rnd in first st (worked into second lobe) of this rnd.

Rnd 7: [Sc in next 6 sts, sc2tog] 4 times—28 sts.

Rnd 8: Sc in each st around.

Rnd 9: [Sc in next 5 sts, sc2tog] 4 times—24 sts.

Rnd 10: [Sc in next 4 sts, sc2tog] 4 times—20 sts.

Begin stuffing heart and continue to stuff until piece is complete.

Rnd 11: [Sc in next 3 sts, sc2tog] 4 times—16 sts.

Rnd 12: [Sc in next 2 sts, sc2tog] 4 times—12 sts.

Rnd 13: Sc in each st around.

Rnd 14: [Sc in next st, sc2tog] 4 times—8 sts.

You may need to use something like the end of a pencil to continue stuffing.

Rnd 15: [Sc2tog] 4 times–4 sts.

Fasten off, leaving a long tail. With tail, sew opening closed. Weave in ends.

Bottle Opening

The bottle neck is worked into the unworked sts of the bottle opening (2 sts on each side of opening) and the 2 holes at the front and back of the opening (see arrows in photo on next page).

Rnd 1: With pink yarn, place a slip knot on hook and work a sc in the hole at the back of the bottle opening, sc again in the same hole, 2 sc in each of next 2 unworked sts of the bottle opening, 2 sc in the hole at the front of the bottle opening, 2 sc in each of the next 2 unworked sts—12 sts.

Rnd 2: [Sc in next st, 2 sc in next st] 6 times—18 sts.

Rnd 3: Working in FLO, sc in each st around.

Fasten off and weave in ends.

Stopper

With black yarn, make a magic ring.

Rnd 1: Work 6 sc into ring; do not join, work in continuous rnds (spiral).

Place a marker in last st made to indicate end of rnd. Move marker up as each rnd is completed.

Rnd 2: 2 sc in each of next 6 sts—12 sts.

Rnd 3: Working in BLO, sc in each st around.

Rnd 4: [Sc in next 2 sts, sc2tog] 3 times—9 sts.

Fasten off, leaving a long tail for sewing.

Stuff the stopper and sew it into the bottle opening using free back loops from Rnd 3 of the heart. The stitch count does not match, so use every other stitch on the heart. *Tip:* Roll the opening down to give you full access to those free back loops.

Magic Mushrooms

Designed by Amanda Sennett of Crochet By A Manda Lorian

Step into an enchanted forest where love blooms and danger lurks behind every tree. These whimsical magic mushrooms add a dose of wonder to any space and are perfect for setting the stage for your next woodland meet-cute.

Skill Level

Measurements

- Smaller mushroom made with worsted weight yarn (#4 medium): measures approx. 3 x 3" (7.5 x 7.5 cm).
- Larger mushroom made with super bulky yarn (#6 super bulky): measures approx. 6 x 6" (15 x 15 cm).

Yarn

- Any weight yarn in stem, mushroom top, and spot colors of your choice.
- *Shown:* Smaller mushroom: I Love This Yarn (7 oz/198 g, 355 yd/324 m, 100% acrylic) in Red (40), White (10), and Gray Mist (200)
- Larger mushroom: Bernat Blanket Yarn (10.5 oz/ 300 g, 220 yd/201 m, 100% polyester) in Pow Purple, Moonlight Sparkle, and Seaside Sparkle
- Less than 1 skein of each color is required.

Crochet Hook

- 2.75 mm (size C/2) crochet hook for worsted weight yarn
- 6 mm (size J/10) crochet hook for super bulky yarn
- *Note:* These are my preferred hook sizes, but you may need to use different sizes if you are prone to loose or tight tension.

Materials

Stuffing

Notions

Scissors
Stitch markers
Tapestry needle

Gauge

Gauge is not critical for this project.

Note

- Do not mix yarn weights. Use the same yarn weight for all three yarn colors.

MUSHROOM STEM AND TOP

With stem color yarn, make a magic ring.

Rnd 1: Work 6 sc into ring; do not join, work in continuous rnds (spiral).

Place a marker in last st made to indicate end of rnd. Move marker up as each rnd is completed.

Rnd 2: 2 sc in each of next 6 sts—12 sts.

Rnd 3: Working in BLO, sc in each st around.

Rnd 4: Sc in each st around.

Rnd 5: [Sc in next 4 sts, sc2tog] 2 times—10 sts.

Rnd 6: Sc in each st around.

Begin stuffing the stem. Manipulate the stuffing so the stem is stuffed firmly, but the first 2 rounds are either flat or inverted. This will allow the mushroom to stand when finished.

Rnd 7: [Sc in next 3 sts, sc2tog] 2 times—8 sts.

Rnds 8–12: Sc in each st around (5 rnds).

Stop stuffing. No stuffing will be needed past this point.

Rnd 13: 2 dc in each st around—16 sts.

Rnd 14: 2 dc in each st around—32 sts; remove the end of rnd marker, hdc in next st. This will even out the rnd and is the new end of rnd. Replace the end of rnd marker.

Change to mushroom top color yarn.

Rnd 15: Working in FLO, [sc in next st, 2 sc in next st] 16 times—48 sts. *Note:* It may be helpful to use stitch markers to mark the first and last free back loops of this rnd. You will remove the markers after Rnd 19.

Rnds 16 and 17: Sc in each st around (2 rnds).

Rnd 18: [Sc in next st, sc2tog] 16 times—32 sts.

Rnd 19: Working through both loops of Rnd 18 and free back loops of Rnd 15, sc in each st around.

Rnd 20: [Sc in next 2 sts, sc2tog] 8 times—24 sts.

Rnd 21: [Sc in next 2 sts, sc2tog] 6 times—18 sts.

Rnd 22: Sc in each st around.

Rnd 23: [Sc in next st, sc2tog] 6 times—12 sts.

Fasten off, leaving a long tail for closing the top of mushroom. Weave tail back and forth through the front loops of Rnd 23, pulling tight to close the hole. Tie off and hide the tail inside the top of the mushroom.

Scan to watch a video tutorial on how to work two rounds together in Round 19.

SPOTS

With spot color yarn, make a magic ring.

Rnd 1: Work 6 sc into ring; sl st in next st.

Fasten off, leaving a long tail for sewing.

Make as many spots as you want and sew them to the top of the mushroom.

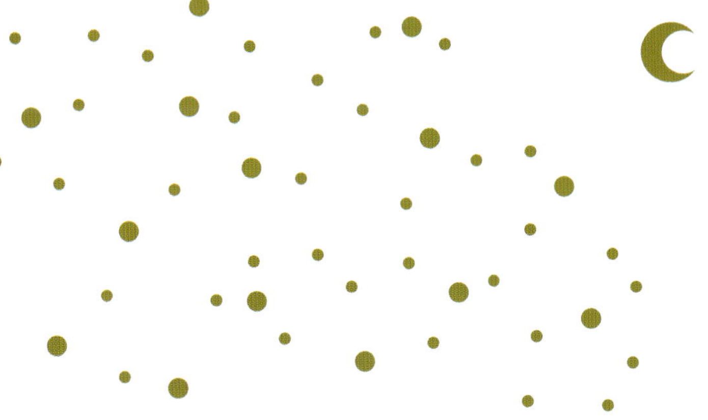

Dragon-Eyed Chalice

Designed by Amanda Sennett of Crochet By A Manda Lorian

This dragon-eyed chalice is destined for raising a drink to those beloved side characters whose tragic deaths we will *never* recover from. Fierce and fun, it's ready to hold your drink as you mourn their painful loss—or raise it high to celebrate the plot twist you didn't see coming.

Skill Level

Measurements

- Cup made with bulky weight yarn (#5 bulky): measures approx. 9" (23 cm) tall.

Yarn

- Bulky weight yarn (#5 bulky) in gray, gold (optional), and black (optional)
- *Shown:* Yarn Bee Velvety Smooth (3.5 oz/100 g, 80 yd/73 m, 100% polyester) in Counting Cloud (9)
- Less than 1 skein of each color is required.
- Bernat Velvet (10.5 oz/300 g, 315 yd/288 m, 100% polyester) in Golden Moss and Blackbird (optional) if choosing to crochet dragon eye
- Scrap amounts of each color are required.

Crochet Hook

- 5 mm (size H/8). *Note:* This is my preferred hook size, but you may need to use a different size if you are prone to loose or tight tension.

Materials

Stuffing
Slit-pupil safety eye (optional) if choosing not to crochet the dragon eye

Notions

Scissors
Stitch markers
Tapestry needle

Gauge

Gauge is not critical for this project.

Special Stitch

- **I-Cord Stitch:** Leaving a starting tail twice the length of desired cord, make a slipknot. Wrap the tail around the hook, then pull working yarn through both loops on the hook. Repeat until cord reaches desired length.

BASE AND STEM

With gray yarn, make a magic ring.

Rnd 1: Work 6 sc into ring; do not join, work in continuous rnds (spiral).

Place a marker in last st made to indicate end of rnd. Move marker up as each rnd is completed.

Rnd 2: 2 sc in each of next 6 sts—12 sts.

Rnd 3: Working in FLO, [sc in next st, 2 sc in next st] 6 times—18 sts. Place a marker in the first and last front loop of this rnd so it's easier to see them later when working Rnd 12.

Rnd 4: [Sc in next 2 sts, 2 sc in next st] 6 times—24 sts.

Rnd 5: [Sc in next 3 sts, 2 sc in next st] 6 times—30 sts.

Rnd 6: [Sc in next 4 sts, 2 sc in next st] 6 times—36 sts.

Rnd 7: Working in BLO, sc in each st around.

Rnd 8: Working in BLO, [sc in next 4 sts, sc2tog] 6 times—30 sts.

Rnd 9: [Sc in next 3 sts, sc2tog] 6 times—24 sts.

Rnd 10: [Sc in next 2 sts, sc2tog] 6 times—18 sts.

Rnd 11: [Sc in next st, sc2tog] 6 times—12 sts.

Rnd 12: Working through both loops of sts in Rnd 11 AND the free back loops from Rnd 3, sc in each st around. This will create a concave disc and forms the bottom of the chalice.

Rnd 13: [Sc in next 2 sts, sc2tog] 3 times—9 sts.

Rnd 14: Sc in each st around.

Rnd 15: [Sc in next st, sc2tog] 3 times—6 sts.

Rnds 16–18: Sc in each st around (3 rnds).

Begin firmly stuffing the stem of the chalice and continue stuffing as you go.

Rnd 19: [Sc in next st, 2 sc in next st] 3 times—9 sts.

Rnd 20: [Sc in next 2 sts, 2 sc in next st] 3 times—12 sts.

Rnds 21 and 22: Sc in each st around (2 rnds).

Rnd 23: [Sc in next 2 sts, sc2tog] 3 times—9 sts.

Rnd 24: Working in FLO, 2 sc in each st around—18 sts.

Invisible fasten off, leaving a long tail for sewing.

Scan to watch a video tutorial on how to work two rounds together in Round 12 of the Base and Stem.

CUP

With gray yarn, make a magic ring.

Rnd 1: Work 6 sc into ring; do not join, work in continuous rnds (spiral).

Place a marker in last st made to indicate end of rnd. Move marker up as each rnd is completed.

Rnd 2: Work 2 sc in each of next 6 sts—12 sts.

Rnd 3: [Sc in next st, 2 sc in next st] 6 times—18 sts.

Rnd 4: [Sc in next 2 sts, 2 sc in next st] 6 times—24 sts.

Rnd 5: [Sc in next 3 sts, 2 sc in next st] 6 times—30 sts.

Rnd 6: [Sc in next 4 sts, 2 sc in next st] 6 times—36 sts.

Rnd 7: [Sc in next 5 sts, 2 sc in next st] 6 times—42 sts.

Rnds 8–15: Sc in each st around (8 rnds).

Invisible fasten off and hide loose ends.

Sew starting rounds of the cup onto the open end of the stem using the ending tail from the stem.

DRAGON EYE APPLIQUÉ (OPTIONAL)

With gold yarn, ch 2.

Row 1: Sc in 2nd ch from hook, turn—1 st.

Row 2: Ch 1, 2 sc in st, turn—2 sts.

Row 3: Ch 1, 2 sc in each of next 2 sts, turn—4 sts.

Row 4: Ch 1, sc in each st across, turn.

Row 5: Ch 1, [sc2tog] 2 times, turn—2 sts.

Row 6: Ch 1, sc2tog, turn—1 st.

Row 7: Ch 1, sc in st.

Fasten off, leaving a long tail for sewing.

With black scrap yarn, sew through the center of the eye between Rows 4 and 5 to create the slit pupil.

Upper Eyelid

With gray yarn and using the I-Cord Stitch (see page 39), stitch 12 and fasten off with a tail for sewing.

Scan to watch a video tutorial on the I-Cord Stitch used for the upper eyelid.

Lower Eyelid

With gray yarn, ch 8.

Fasten off, leaving a long tail for sewing.

ASSEMBLY

1. Sew eyes at an angle between Rnds 9 and 11 of cup. If you are using safety eyes, attach them in Rnd 10 of cup.
2. Sew upper eyelid along top edge of the eye, extending past the outer corner of the eye.
3. Sew lower eyelid along bottom edge of the eye, with ends at each corner.

Tribute Roses

Designed by Amanda Sennett of Crochet By A Manda Lorian

Not every love is easy—some are thorny, dangerous, and filled with sacrifice. These crochet roses pay homage to those epic romances where nothing comes easily. From classic tales of enchanted roses to epic quests where a rose symbolizes the heart's deepest struggles, this floral icon is ever-present. Create your own version of the timeless symbol with this pattern.

Skill Level

Measurements

- Rose made with worsted weight yarn (#4 medium): measures approx. 4" (10 cm) long.
- Rose made with bulky weight yarn (#5 bulky): measures approx. 6" (15 cm) long.
- Rose made with super bulky weight yarn (#6 super bulky): measures approx. 8" (20.5 cm) long.

Yarn

- Any weight yarn in rose petal color of your choice and green.
- *Shown:* I Love This Yarn (7 oz/198 g, 355 yd/324 m, 100% acrylic) in Red (40) and Dark Olive (130)
- Bernat Velvet Yarn (10.5 oz/300 g, 315 yd/288 m, 100% polyester) in Red and Pine
- Bernat Blanket Yarn (10.5 oz/300 g, 220 yd/201 m, 100% polyester) in Crimson and Smokey Green
- Less than 1 skein of each color is required.

Crochet Hook

- 2.75 mm (size C/2) for worsted weight yarn
- 3.75 mm (size F/5) for bulky weight yarn
- 6 mm (size J/10) for super bulky weight yarn
- *Note:* These are my preferred hook sizes, but you may need to use different sizes if you are prone to loose or tight tension.

Materials

Stuffing (optional)
Dowel (optional)

Notions

Scissors
Stitch markers
Tapestry needle

Gauge

Gauge is not critical for this project.

Notes

- Do not mix yarn weights. Use the same yarn weight for all three yarn colors.
- Get creative with colors and textures—my favorite is Bernat Velvet yarn, which adds a beautiful shine to the petals, perfect for capturing both the softness and resilience of love.

PETALS (MAKE 9)

With rose color yarn, make a magic ring.

Rnd 1: Work 6 sc into ring; do not join, work in continuous rnds (spiral).

Place a marker in last st made to indicate end of rnd. Move marker up as each rnd is completed.

Rnd 2: 2 sc in each of next 6 sts—12 sts.

Rnd 3: 2 sc in each of next 12 sts—24 sts.

Invisible fasten off. Weave in tails.

BASE

With rose color yarn, leaving a long beginning tail.

Rnds 1–3: Work same as Rnds 1–3 of petals—24 sts in Rnd 3.

JOIN PETALS TO BASE

Rnd 4: * Hold base and one petal with WS together and next 3 sts matching; working through both thicknesses, sc in next 3 sts; rep from * attaching a new petal each time until 8 petals have been joined around base. *Note:* The 9th petal will be used later.

Fasten off, leaving a long tail for sewing.

Scan to watch a video tutorial on how to connect the petals.

STEM

With green yarn, make a magic ring.

Rnd 1: Work 5 sc into ring; do not join, work in continuous rnds (spiral).

There is no need for an end of rnd marker when working the stem.

Rnd 2: Sc in each st around.

Rep Rnd 2 until stem reaches desired length.

Stuff if you like, or you can insert a wooden dowel inside the stem if you want the flower to be rigid.

Next rnd: Working in FLO, 2 sc in each st around—10 sts.

Next rnd: 2 sc in each st around—20 sts.

Next rnd: [Sc in next st, dc in next st, ch 2, sl st in 2nd ch from hook, dc in same st as previous dc, sc in next 2 sts] 5 times—25 sts.

Fasten off, leaving a tail for sewing.

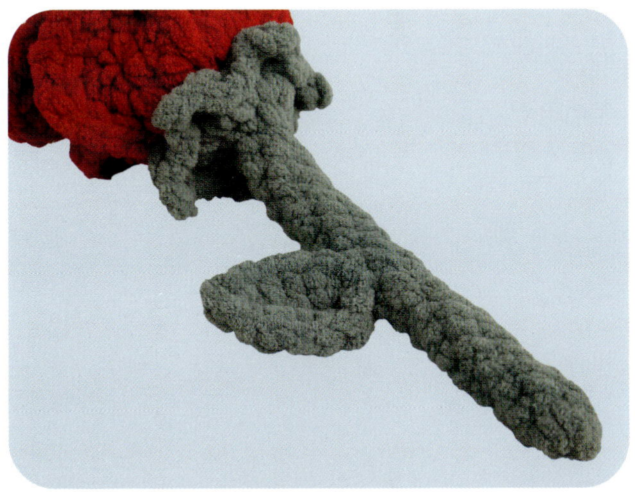

LEAF

With green yarn, ch 6.

Row 1: Sl st in 2nd ch from hook, sc in next ch, hdc in next ch, dc in next ch, (hdc, 2 sc, hdc) all in last ch; working along opposite side of foundation ch, dc in next ch, hdc in next ch, sc in next ch, sl st in next ch.

Fasten off, leaving a tail for sewing.

ASSEMBLY

1. Carefully twist the petals into position to resemble a rose.
2. Roll the 9th petal into a cone and use the beginning tail from the base to sew it into the center. The rest of the petals should wrap around it one by one in a spiral.
3. Using the long ending tail from the base, sew through the inside of the petals all the way around to keep them wrapped around the center. Feed the yarn tail out through the bottom of the flower to secure to the stem. At this point, I like to push the bottom of the rose up to be an inverted cone, leaving the entirety of Rnd 4 of the base as the bottom edge of the flower. This is the round you will be sewing down onto the stem.
4. Using both the tails from the flower and the stem, sew the flower onto the wide part of the stem. Hide both tails inside the stem.
5. Sew the leaf onto the stem.

Now you have your very own artificial rose that will never wilt or cut you with its thorns!

Skeleton Keys

Designed by Staci Burns of Fiddlesticks Crochet

Unlock the mysteries of your heart with these skeleton keys. You never know what the keys might open—whether a chest of hidden desires or the door to a forgotten realm. With each turn, they could reveal the path to love, danger, or something entirely unexpected.

Skill Level

Measurements

- Key made with worsted weight yarn (#4 medium): measures approx. 7¾" (19.5 cm).
- Key made with size 10 crochet cotton: measures approx. 3½" (9 cm).

Yarn

- Any weight yarn in silver
- *Shown:* Lion Brand Pound of Love (16 oz/454 g, 1,020 yd/932 m, 100% premium acrylic) in Maize (39)
- Aunt Lydia's Size 10 Metallic Crochet Thread (100 yd/91 m, 93% cotton, 6% metallic) in Silver/Silver
- Less than 1 skein of each color is required.

Crochet Hook

- 2.75 mm (size C/2) for worsted weight yarn
- 1.50 mm steel for size 10 crochet cotton
- *Note:* These are my preferred hook sizes, but you may need to use different sizes if you are prone to loose or tight tension.

Materials

Stuffing
Fabric stiffener (optional)

Notions

Scissors
Stitch markers
Tapestry needle

Gauge

Gauge is not critical for this project.

BARREL

Make a magic ring.

Rnd 1: Work 6 sc into ring; do not join, work in continuous rnds (spiral).

Place a marker in last st made to indicate end of rnd. Move marker up as each rnd is completed.

Rnd 2: [Sc in next st, 2 sc in next st] 3 times—9 sts.

Rnd 3: Working in BLO, sc in each st around.

Begin stuffing barrel and continue stuffing until piece is complete.

Rnds 4–14: Sc in each st around (11 rnds).

Rnd 15: 2 sc in each st around—18 sts.

Rnd 16: Sc in each st around.

Rnd 17: [Sc2tog] 9 times—9 sts.

Rnds 18–31: Sc in each st around (14 rnds).

Fasten off, leaving a long tail. With tail, sew opening closed.

BIG BOW PIECES (MAKE 2)

Make a magic ring.

Rnd 1: Work 6 sc into ring; do not join, work in continuous rnds (spiral).

Place a marker in last st made to indicate end of rnd. Move marker up as each rnd is completed.

Rnd 2: Working in BLO, sc in next 6 sts.

Stuff bow lightly and continue stuffing until piece is complete.

Rnds 3–27: Sc in each st around (25 rnds).

Fasten off, leaving a long tail for sewing.

Sew one end of first piece between Rnds 26 and 29 of barrel. Sew other end of first piece to end of barrel. Sew second piece to opposite side of barrel, sewing one end of piece between Rnds 26 and 29 and the other end of piece to end of barrel.

TOP BOW

Make a magic ring.

Rnd 1: Work 6 sc into ring; do not join, work in continuous rnds (spiral).

Place a marker in last st made to indicate end of rnd. Move marker up as each rnd is completed.

Rnd 2: Working in BLO, sc in next 6 sts.

Stuff bow lightly and continue stuffing until piece is complete.

Rnds 3–17: Sc in each st around (15 rnds).

Fasten off, leaving a long tail for sewing.

Sew piece in an arch over the big bows, referring to photos for placement.

BIT

Ch 6.

Row 1: Sc in 2nd ch from hook and in next 4 ch, turn—5 sts.

Row 2: Ch 1, sc in each st across, turn.

Row 3: Ch 1, sl st in first 3 sts, sc in last 2 sts, turn.

Row 4: Ch 1, sc in next 2 sts; leave last 3 sts unworked, turn—2 sts.

Row 5: Ch 1, sc in next 2 sts, turn.

Row 6: Ch 1, sl st in next 2 sts, turn.

Row 7: Ch 4, sc in 2nd ch from hook and in next 2 ch, sc in next 2 sts, turn—5 sts.

Row 8: Ch 1, sc in each st across, turn.

Row 9: Ch 1, sl st in each st across.

Fasten off, leaving a long tail for sewing.

Weave in beginning tail.

Sew bit between Rows 4 and 13 of barrel.

OPTIONAL

Apply fabric stiffener to the surface and lay flat to dry overnight or until dry.

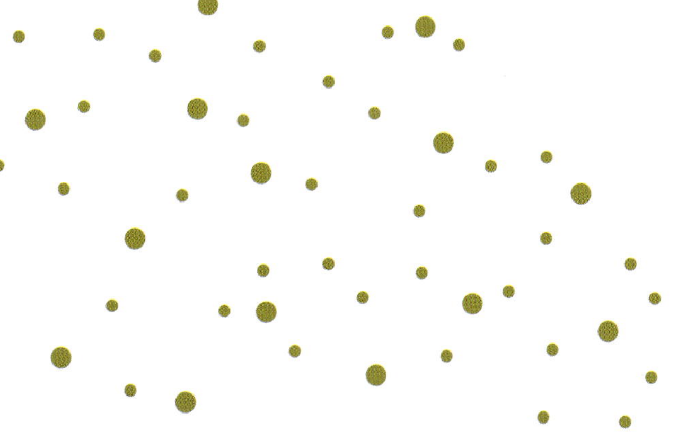

SKULLS

Designed by Amanda Sennett of Crochet By A Manda Lorian

Add a touch of something wicked to your trophy shelf collection with these crocheted skulls. They're perfect for sending secret messages or reminding you that love and danger often walk hand in hand—because what's romantasy without a little brush with death?

Skill Level

Measurements

- Skull made with worsted weight yarn (#4 medium): measures approx. 4 x 4" (10 x 10 cm).
- Skull made with super bulky weight yarn (#6 super bulky): measures approx. 8 x 8" (20.5 x 20.5 cm).

Yarn

- Any weight yarn in white and black.
- *Shown:* I Love This Yarn (7 oz/198 g, 355 yd/324 m, 100% acrylic) in White (10) and Black (30)
- Bernat Blanket Yarn (10.5 oz/300 g, 220 yd/201 m, 100% polyester) in White and Coal
- Less than 1 skein of each color is required.

Crochet Hook

- 2.75 mm (size C/2) for worsted weight yarn
- 6 mm (size J/10) for super bulky weight yarn
- *Note:* These are my preferred hook sizes, but you may need to use different sizes if you are prone to loose or tight tension.

Materials

Stuffing

Notions

Scissors
Stitch markers
Tapestry needle

Gauge

Gauge is not critical for this project.

Note

- Do not mix yarn weights. Use the same yarn weight for both yarn colors.

HEAD

With white yarn, make a magic ring.

Rnd 1: Work 8 sc into ring; do not join, work in continuous rnds (spiral).

Place a marker in last st made to indicate end of rnd. Move marker up as each rnd is completed.

Rnd 2: 2 sc in each of next 8 sts—16 sts.

Rnd 3: [Sc in next st, 2 sc in next st] 8 times—24 sts.

Rnd 4: [Sc in next 3 sts, 2 sc in next st] 6 times—30 sts.

Rnd 5: [Sc in next 4 sts, 2 sc in next st] 6 times—36 sts.

Rnd 6: [Sc in next 5 sts, 2 sc in next st] 6 times—42 sts.

Rnds 7–13: Sc in each st around (7 rnds).

Rnd 14: Working in BLO, sc in next 14 sts; working in both loops, sc in last 28 sts.

Rnd 15: [Sc in next 5 sts, sc2tog] 6 times—36 sts.

Rnd 16: [Sc in next 4 sts, sc2tog] 6 times—30 sts.

Rnd 17: [Sc in next 3 sts, sc2tog] 6 times—24 sts.

Begin stuffing. Avoid over stuffing, which can cause the head to lose its oblong shape.

Rnd 18: [Sc in next 2 sts, sc2tog] 6 times—18 sts.

Rnd 19: [Sc in next st, sc2tog] 6 times—12 sts.

Rnd 20: [Sc2tog] 6 times—6 sts.

Fasten off, leaving a long tail. Thread tail through sts of last rnd and pull to close opening. Tie off and hide tail inside head.

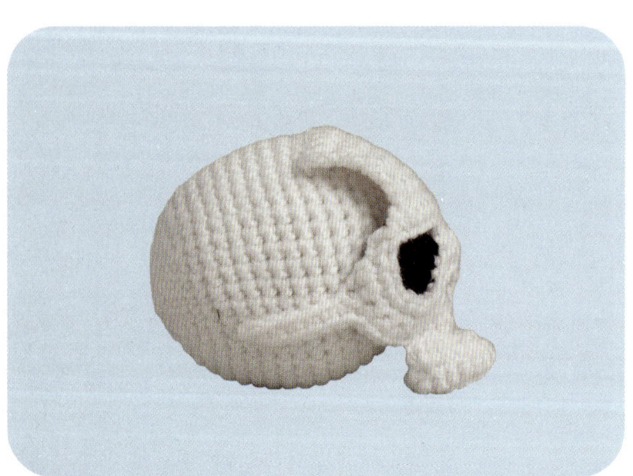

FACE

With white yarn, leaving a long beginning tail for sewing, ch 15.

Row 1: Sc in 2nd ch from hook and in each ch across, turn—14 sc.

Rows 2–8: Ch 1, sc in each st across, turn (7 rows).

Row 9: Ch 1, 2 sc in first st, sc in next 12 sts, 2 sc in last st, turn—16 sts.

Row 10: Ch 1, 2 sc in first st, sc in next 14 sts, 2 sc in last st, turn—18 sts.

Row 11: Ch 1, sc in first st, ch 11, sk next 6 sts, sc in next 4 sts, ch 11, sk next 6 sts, sc in last st, turn—6 sc and 2 ch-11.

Row 12: Ch 1, sc in first st, sc in each ch of next ch-11, dc in next 4 sts, sc in each ch of next ch-11, sc in last st, turn—28 sts.

Row 13: Ch 1, sk first st, sl st in next st, sc in next 8 sts, ch 2, sk next 8 sts, sc in next 8 sts, sl st in next st; leave last st unworked, turn—16 sc and 1 ch-2.

Row 14: Do not ch, sk sl st, sl st in next st, sc in next st, ch 7, sc in 2nd ch from hook and in next 5 ch (for side of jaw), 2 sc in each of next 4 sts, hdc in next st, dc in next st, dc in each ch of next ch-2, dc in next st, hdc in next st, 2 sc in each of next 4 sts, ch 7, sc in 2nd ch from hook and in next 5 ch (for side of jaw), sc in next st, sl st in last st.

Fasten off, leaving an extra-long tail for sewing.

TEETH

With white yarn, make a magic ring.

Row 1: Work 4 sc into ring, turn—4 sts.

Row 2: Ch 1, 2 sc in each st across, turn—8 sts.

Row 3: Ch 1, [sc in next st, 2 sc in next st] 4 times, turn—12 sts.

Row 4: Ch 1, working in FLO, sc in each st across, turn.

Row 5: Ch 1, sc in next st, sc2tog, sc in next 6 sts, sc2tog, sc in next st, turn—10 sts.

Row 6: Ch 1, 2 sc in each of next 2 sts, [sc2tog] 3 times, 2 sc in each of last 2 sts—11 sts.

Fasten off, leaving a long tail for sewing.

EYE HOLES (MAKE 2)

With black yarn, make a magic ring.

Rnd 1: Work 8 sc into ring; do not join, work in continuous rnds (spiral).

Rnd 2: 2 sc in each of next 3 sts, 2 dc in each of next 2 sts, 2 sc in each of last 3 sts—16 sts.

Invisible fasten off, leaving a long tail for sewing.

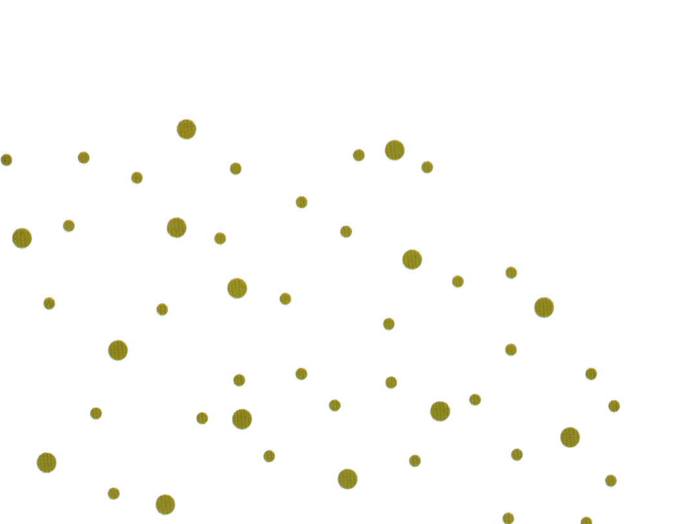

NOSE HOLE

With black yarn, make a magic ring.

Rnd 1: Work 8 sc into ring; do not join, work in continuous rnds (spiral).

Place a marker in last st made to indicate end of rnd.

Rnd 2: Sl st in next st, (dc, tr) in next st, (tr, dc) in next st, sl st in next st; leave remaining sts unworked.

Fasten off, leaving a long tail for sewing.

ASSEMBLY

1. With the tails from the eye holes, sew in place in the larger two holes of the face.
2. With the tail from the nose hole, sew in place in the smaller hole of the face.
3. With the tail from the teeth, sew underneath the nose hole, making sure it is centered.
4. With the beginning tail from the face, sew in place along the front loops left over from Rnd 14 of the head.
5. Weave in all remaining ends, leaving only the tail from the face for the next step.
6. With the ending tail from the face, pull the sides of the jaw from Row 14 to the sides of the head, sew them down, and hide the rest of the tail inside the head.
7. There will be some gapping between the face and the head because that is how a real skull looks, but if you don't like that look, you can sew the face panel all the way down.

If you want to add teeth outlines, use a strand of black yarn and sew hash marks across the bottom of the teeth area.

Now death can grace your bookshelf!

Dagger & Sword

Designed by Amanda Sennett of Crochet By A Manda Lorian

Every heroine needs a weapon, and no enemies-to-lovers story is complete without a bit of swordplay. Whether you're a *violent little thing* defending your own heart or battling to save the world, these crocheted daggers and swords show you can take care of yourself—with a wicked edge.

Skill Level

Measurements

- Dagger made with worsted weight yarn (#4 medium): measures approx. 12" (30.5 cm) long.
- Sword made with bulky weight yarn (#5 bulky): measures approx. 36" (91.5 cm) long.

Yarn

- Worsted weight yarn (#4 medium) in gray and black for dagger.
- Bulky weight yarn (#5 bulky) in gray and black for sword.
- *Shown:* I Love This Yarn (7 oz/198 g, 355 yd/324 m, 100% acrylic) in Gray Mist (200) and Black (30)
- Bernat Blanket Yarn (10.5 oz/300 g, 220 yd/201 m, 100% polyester) in Vapor Gray and Coal
- Less than 1 skein of each color is required for each piece.

Crochet Hook

- 2.75 mm (size C/2) for worsted weight yarn
- 6 mm (size J/10) for bulky weight yarn
- *Note:* These are my preferred hook sizes, but you may need to use different sizes if you are prone to loose or tight tension.

Materials

- Stuffing
- ¼" (6 mm) wooden dowel cut to 11" (28 cm) long (optional for dagger)
- Yard stick or meter stick (for sword)

Notions

Scissors
Stitch markers
Tapestry needle

Gauge

Gauge is not critical for this project.

Notes

- Do not mix yarn weights. Use the same yarn weight for both yarn colors.
- Make a dagger you can use as a prop by inserting a dowel for rigidity, or stuff lightly if the dagger will just be used as décor.

DAGGER

Dagger Blade Panels (make 2)

With gray yarn, ch 2.

Row 1: Sc in 2nd ch from hook, turn—1 st.

Row 2: Ch 1, 2 sc in next st, turn—2 sts.

Row 3: Ch 1, 2 sc in next st, sc in last st, turn—3 sts.

Row 4: Ch 1, sc in next st, 2 sc in next st, sc in last, turn—4 sts.

Rows 5–34: Ch 1, sc in each st across, turn (30 rows).

Fasten off first panel. Do not fasten off second panel.

Join Dagger Blade Panels

Place first panel on top of second panel with stitches and ends of rows matching.

Working through both thicknesses, work 34 sc evenly spaced alongside edge to beginning point, 2 sc in point, ch 2, sl st in 2nd ch from hook, 2 sc in same point (hide the yarn tails inside the tip of the dagger here), work 34 sc evenly spaced down second side of piece; do not work across lower end.

Fasten off.

If you are using a dowel, carefully insert it between the panels all the way to the point. Set the blade aside for now. It will be crocheted in place after making hilt.

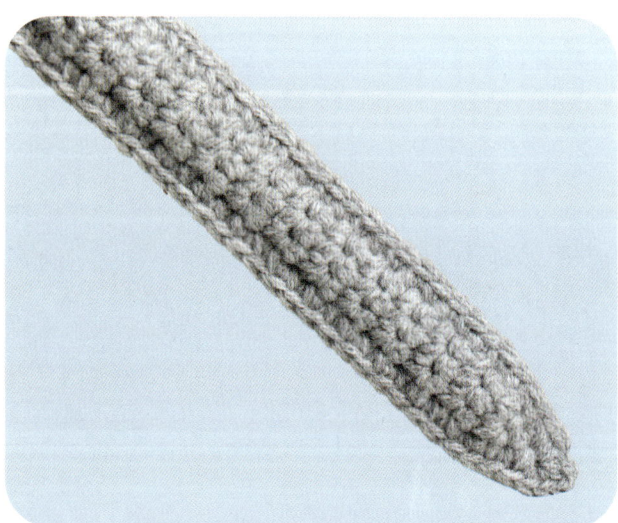

Dagger Hilt

With black yarn, make a magic ring.

Rnd 1: Work 3 sc into ring; do not join, work in continuous rnds (spiral).

Place a marker in last st made to indicate end of rnd. Move marker up as each rnd is completed.

Rnd 2: 2 sc in each of next 3 sts—6 sts.

Rnd 3: [Sc in next st, 2 sc in next st] 3 times—9 sts.

Rnd 4: [Sc in next 2 sts, 2 sc in next st] 3 times—12 sts.

Rnd 5: [Sc in next 3 sts, 2 sc in next st] 3 times—15 sts.

Rnd 6: [Sc in next 4 sts, 2 sc in next st] 3 times—18 sts.

Rnd 7: [Sc in next 2 sts, 2 sc in next st] 6 times—24 sts.

Rnd 8: Sk next 6 sts, sc in next 6 sts, sk next 6 sts, sc in last 6 sts—12 sts.

This will form a flattened cone shape that will be the bottom of the hilt.

Rnds 9–26: Sc in each st around (18 rnds).

Rnd 27: 2 sc in each st around—24 sts.

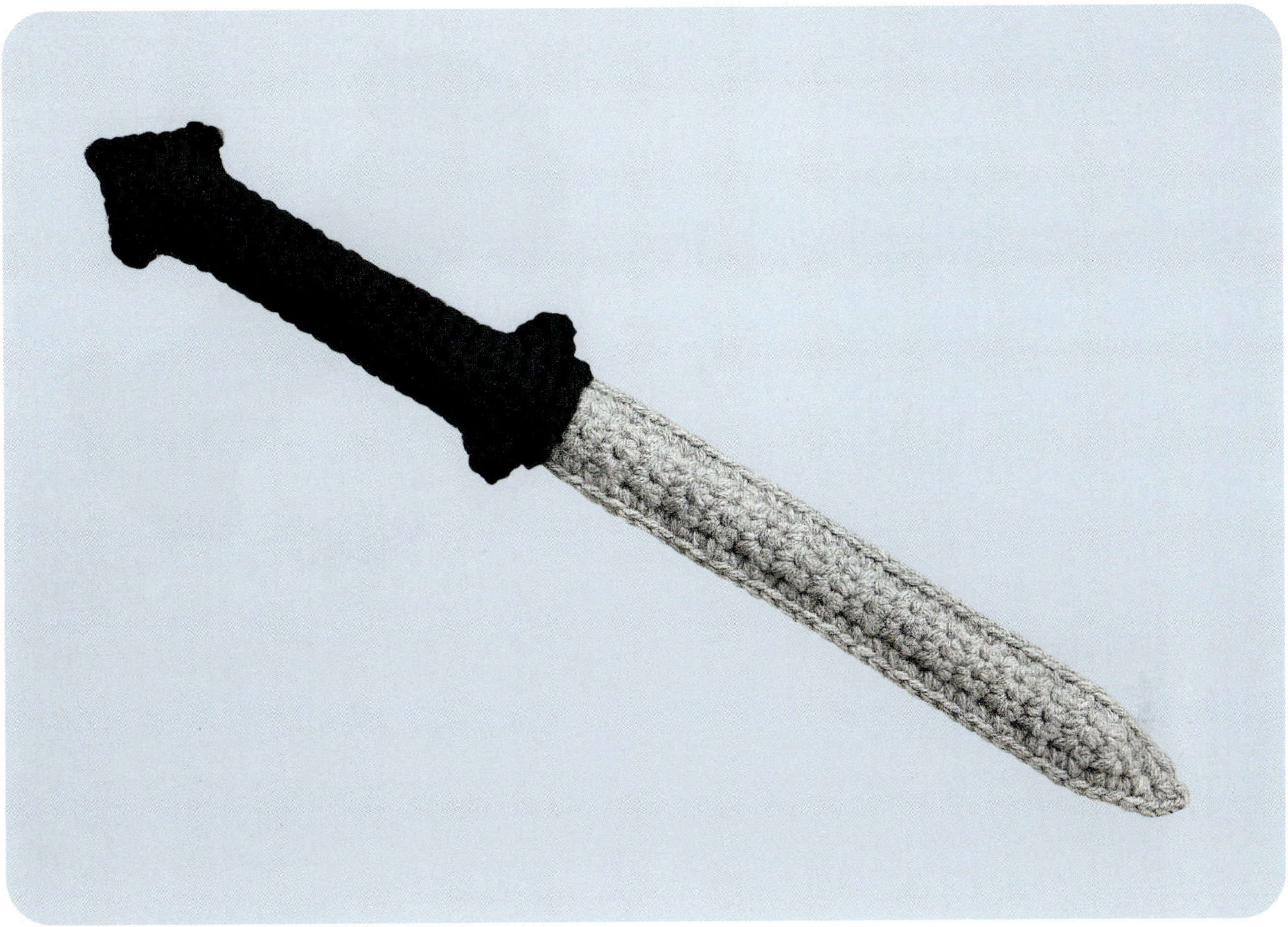

Attach Dagger Blade to Hilt

The last st you made should be in the middle of one side of the hilt (halfway between the openings created in Rnd 8). Work another sc or two if you're not in the middle.

Slide the hilt onto the exposed end of the dowel and make sure the blade and hilt are just about touching. The open end of the blade should be facing you along with the side of the hilt with the working yarn attached.

Add some stuffing on either side of the dowel if the hilt doesn't feel filled out. You can add stuffing through the open end and the holes created in Rnd 8.

You will now work through both layers (hilt and blade) to join hilt to blade. When working into blade, work 1 st into each sc and 2 sts in each seam between panels (for a total of 12 sts).

Rnd 28: Beginning in 3rd sc of one side of blade panel and working through both thicknesses (hilt and blade), sc in next 3 sts, sk next 6 sts of hilt only; working through both thicknesses, sc in next 6 sts; sk next 6 sts of hilt only; working through both thicknesses, sc in last 3 sts.

Fasten off and weave in ends.

Using scrap black yarn, sew closed the holes in the hilt created in Rnds 8 and 28.

Scan to watch a video tutorial on how to attach the hilt to the blade.

SWORD

Sword Blade Panels (make 2)

With gray yarn, ch 2.

Row 1: Sc in 2nd ch from hook, turn—1 st.

Row 2: Ch 1, 2 sc in next st, turn—2 sts.

Row 3: Ch 1, 2 sc in next st, sc in last st, turn—3 sts.

Row 4: Ch 1, sc in next st, 2 sc in next st, sc in last, turn—4 sts.

Row 5: Ch 1, sc in each st across, turn (68 rows).

Rep Row 5 until blade measures about 32" (81.5 cm) from beginning.

Fasten off first panel. Do not fasten off second panel.

Join Sword Blade Panels

Place first panel on top of second panel with stitches and ends of rows matching.

Working through both thicknesses, work 72 sc evenly spaced along side edge to beginning point, 2 sc in point, ch 2, sl st in 2nd ch from hook, 2 sc in same point (hide the yarn tails inside the tip of the sword here), work 72 sc evenly spaced down second side of piece; do not work across lower end.

Fasten off.

Carefully slide the yard stick into the blade, working stick slowly and carefully so the pointed corners don't snag stitches. The top of the yard stick should sit right at Row 5 of the blade. Set the blade aside for now. It will be crocheted in place after making hilt.

Sword Hilt

With black yarn, make a magic ring.

Rnd 1: Work 8 sc into ring; do not join, work in continuous rnds (spiral).

Place a marker in last st made to indicate end of rnd. Move marker up as each rnd is completed.

Rnd 2: 2 sc in each of next 8 sts—16 sts.

Rnd 3: [Sc in next st, 2 sc in next st] 8 times—24 sts.

Rnds 4 and 5: Sc in each st around.

Rnd 6: Sk next 6 sts, sc in next 6 sts, sk next 6 sts, sc in last 6 sts—12 sts.

This will form a flattened semi-circle that will be the bottom of the hilt.

Rnds 7–19: Sc in each st around (13 rnds).

Rnd 20: 2 sc in each st around—24 sts.

Rnd 21: Sc in each st around.

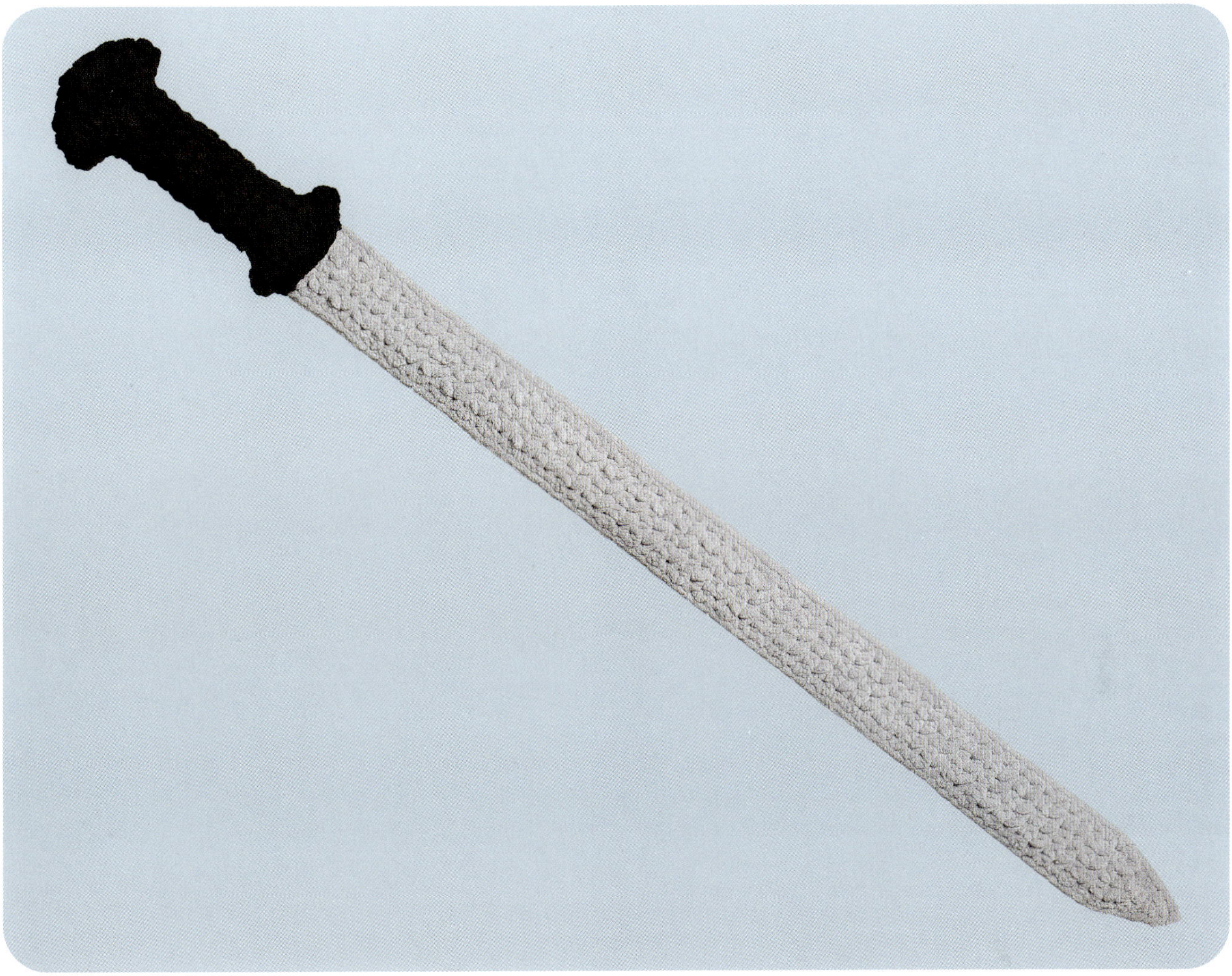

Attach Sword Blade to Hilt

The last st you made should be in the middle of the hilt (halfway between the openings created in Rnd 6). Work another sc or two if you're not in the middle. In the next rnd you will be stitching the hilt to the blade.

Slide the hilt onto the exposed end of yard stick. If you want to have a rounded hilt, add some stuffing on either side of the yard stick. You can add stuffing through the open end and the holes created in Rnd 6.

You will now work through both layers (hilt and blade) to join hilt to blade. When working into blade, work 1 st into each sc and 2 sts in each seam between panels (for a total of 12 sts).

Rnd 22: Beginning in 3rd sc of one side of blade panel and working through both thicknesses (blade and hilt), sc in next 3 sts, sk next 6 sts of hilt only; working through both thicknesses, sc in next 6 sts; sk next 6 sts of hilt only; working through both thicknesses, sc in last 3 sts.

Fasten off and weave in ends.

Using scrap black yarn, sew closed the holes in the hilt created in Rnds 6 and 22.

Now you can show off your skills with a blade large or small!

Scan to watch a video tutorial on how to attach the hilt to the blade.

Enemies-to-Lovers Pierced Hearts

Designed by Amanda Sennett of Crochet By A Manda Lorian

The ultimate tribute to the most popular trope of them all: enemies to lovers! These pierced hearts symbolize the fiery tension, the banter, and, ultimately, the passion that keeps us all hooked.

Skill Level

Measurements

- Heart made with worsted weight yarn (#4 medium): measures approx. 3 x 3" (7.5 x 7.5 cm).
- Heart made with super bulky weight yarn (#6 super bulky): measures approx. 7 x 7" (18 x 18 cm).

Yarn

- Any weight yarn in red, black, and gray.
- *Shown:* I Love This Yarn (7 oz/198 g, 355 yd/324 m, 100% acrylic) in Red (40), Black (30), and Gray Mist (200)
- Bernat Blanket Yarn (10.5 oz/300 g, 220 yd/201 m, 100% polyester) in Crimson, Coal, and Vapor Gray
- Less than 1 skein of each color is required.

Crochet Hook

- 2.75 mm (size C/2) for worsted weight yarn
- 6 mm (size J/10) for bulky weight yarn
- *Note:* These are my preferred hook sizes, but you may need to use different sizes if you are prone to loose or tight tension.

Materials

Stuffing

Notions

Scissors
Stitch markers
Tapestry needle

Gauge

Gauge is not critical for this project.

Note

- Do not mix yarn weights. Use the same yarn weight for all three yarn colors.

HEART LOBES (MAKE 2)

With red yarn, make a magic ring.

Rnd 1: Work 6 sc into ring; do not join, work in continuous rnds (spiral).

Place a marker in last st made to indicate end of rnd. Move marker up as each rnd is completed.

Rnd 2: 2 sc in each of next 6 sts—12 sts.

Rnd 3: [Sc in next st, 2 sc in next st] 6 times—18 sts.

Rnd 4: Sc in each st around.

Invisible fasten off first lobe, leaving a long tail. Make sure when you connect the pieces later that this tail stays on the outside of the heart.

Do not fasten off second lobe.

JOIN LOBES

Rnd 5: Hold lobes together, sc in each st of first lobe then sc in each st of second lobe—36 sts.

Rnd 6: Sc in next 4 sts, [sc2tog, sc in next 2 sts] 2 times, sc2tog, sc in next 8 sts, [sc2tog, sc in next 2 sts] 2 times, sc2tog, sc in last 4 sts—30 sts.

Rnd 7: Sc in each st around.

Rnd 8: Sc in next 4 sts, [sc2tog, sc in next st] 2 times, sc2tog, sc in next 7 sts, [sc2tog, sc in next st] 2 times, sc2tog, sc in last 3 sts—24 sts.

Rnd 9: Sc in each st around.

Begin stuffing lightly. Too much stuffing will make it difficult to pass the knife through the heart later.

Rnd 10: Sc in next 3 sts, [sc2tog] 3 times, sc in next 6 sts, [sc2tog] 3 times, sc in last 3 sts—18 sts.

Rnd 11: Sc in each st around.

Rnd 12: [Sc2tog, sc in next st] 6 times—12 sts.

Rnd 13: Sc in each st around.

Rnd 14: [Sc2tog] 6 times—6 sts.

Fasten off, leaving a long tail for sewing, but DO NOT sew the bottom hole closed yet.

KNIFE HANDLE

With black yarn, make a magic ring.

Rnd 1: Work 4 sc into ring; do not join, work in continuous rnds (spiral).

Place a marker in last st made to indicate end of rnd. Move marker up as each rnd is completed.

Rnds 2–4: Sc in each st around (3 rnds).

Rnd 5: Sc in next st, ch 4, sc in 2nd ch from hook and next 2 ch, sc in next 2 sts, ch 4, sc in 2nd ch from hook and next 2 ch, sl st in next st—9 sts (not including the sl st).

Fasten off and hide the ends inside the handle.

KNIFE BLADE

With gray yarn, leaving a long beginning tail, ch 2.

Row 1: Sc in 2nd ch from hook, turn—1 sts.

Row 2: Ch 1, 2 sc in next st, turn—2 sts.

Row 3: Ch 1, sc in each st across, turn—2 sts.

Rep Row 3 until blade is long enough that it will stick out of the top and bottom of the heart when assembled.

Fasten off, leaving a long tail for sewing.

ASSEMBLY

1. With the ending tail of the knife blade, sew the blade to the handle and hide the ends.
2. With the beginning tail of the knife blade, pass the blade through the top opening (between the lobes) in the heart and out the bottom of the heart. You can use a long needle to separate the stuffing inside the heart to make it easier for the knife to pass through.
3. Once the knife is through the heart, use the tails left at the top and bottom of the heart to sew the blade in place and close the heart's holes around the blade.

And now we've reached the point for which we all wait, not-so-patiently! The enemies have become lovers, and we can finally get some sleep!

3

Wear the Fantasy

Fairy-Tale Mask

Designed by Staci Burns of Fiddlesticks Crochet

Inspired to promenade at a masquerade or to charm your way through the royal court? This fairy-tale mask will have you feeling like the lead in your own magical love story. Bonus points if you lock eyes with someone mysterious across the ballroom.

Skill Level

Measurements

- Mask made with size 10 crochet cotton: measures approx. 7¾" (19.5 cm) across.

Yarn

- Any weight yarn in yarn color of your choice
- *Shown:* Aunt Lydia's Size 10 Metallic Crochet Thread (100 yd/91 m, 93% cotton, 6% metallic) in Silver/Silver
- Less than 1 skein of each color is required.

Crochet Hook

- 1.50 mm steel for size 10 crochet cotton. *Note:* This is my preferred hook size, but you may need to use a different size if you are prone to loose or tight tension.

Materials

Fiber stiffener (optional)
Plastic masquerade mask (optional)

Notions

Scissors
Stitch markers
Tapestry needle

Gauge

Gauge is not critical for this project.

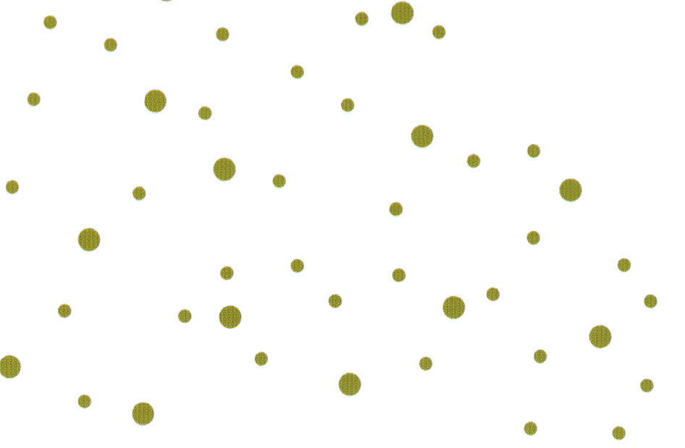

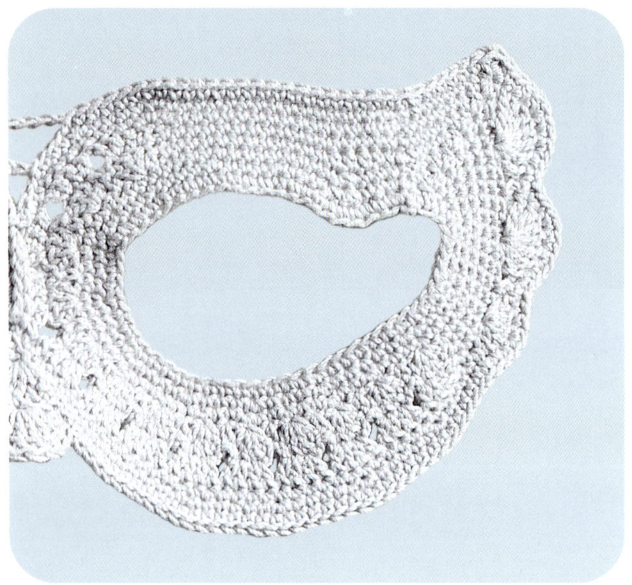

LEFT EYE

Ch 60; join with sl st in back bump of first ch to form a large circle.

Rnd 1 (RS): Ch 1, working in back bumps only, sc in same ch as joining sl st, sc in next 58 ch, (hdc, dc, hdc) in next ch; join with sl st in first sc—62 sts.

Rnd 2: Ch 1, sc in same st as joining sl st, sc in next 2 sts, [sc2tog] 2 times, [sc in next 3 sts, 2 sc in next st] 9 times, sc in next 17 sts, (hdc, dc, hdc) in next st, sc in next st; join with sl st in first sc—71 sts.

Rnd 3: Ch 1, sc in same st as joining sl st, sc in next 2 sts, sc2tog, sc in next 15 sts, [sc in next 2 sts, 2 sc in next st] 11 times, [sc in next 3 sts, 2 sc in next st] 3 times, sc in next 3 sts, (hdc, dc, hdc) in next st, sc in next 2 sts; join with sl st in first sc—86 sts.

Rnd 4: Ch 1, sc in same st as joining sl st, sc in next st, hdc in next 3 sts, sc in next 12 sts, [sk next st, 4 dc in next st, sk next st, sc in next st] 13 times, sc in next 13 sts, (hdc, dc, hdc) in next st, sc in next 3 sts; join with sl st in first sc—101 sts.

Rnd 5: Ch 1, sc in same st as joining sl st, sc in next 16 sts, sk next st, [2 dc in each of next 2 sts, sk next 3 sts] 12 times, 2 dc in each of next 2 sts, sk next st, sc in next 15 sts, (hdc, dc, hdc) in next st, sc in next 4 sts; join with sl st in first sc—91 sts.

Fasten off and weave in ends.

RIGHT EYE

Ch 60; join with sl st in back bump of first ch to form a large circle.

Rnd 1 (RS): Ch 1, working in back bumps only, (hdc, dc, hdc) in same ch as joining sl st, sc in next 59 ch; join with sl st in first hdc—62 sts.

Rnd 2: Ch 1, sc in same st as joining sl st, (hdc, dc, hdc) in next st, sc in next 17 sts, [2 sc in next st, sc in next 3 sts] 9 times, [sc2tog] twice, sc in next 3 sts; join with sl st in first sc—71 sts.

Rnd 3: Ch 1, sc in same st as joining sl st, sc in next st, (hdc, dc, hdc) in next st, sc in next 3 sts, [2 sc in next st, sc in next 3 sts] 3 times, [2 sc in next st, sc in next 2 sts] 11 times, sc in next 15 sts, sc2tog, sc in next 3 sts; join with sl st in first sc—86 sts.

Rnd 4: Ch 1, sc in same st as joining sl st, sc in next 2 sts, (hdc, dc, hdc) in next st, sc in next 13 sts, [sc in next st, sk next st, 4 dc in next st, sk next st] 13 times, sc in next 12 sts, hdc in next 3 sts, sc in next 2 sts; join with sl st in first sc—101 sts.

Rnd 5: Ch 1, sc in same st as joining sl st, sc in next 3 sts, (hdc, dc, hdc) in next st, sc in next 15 sts, sk next st, [2 dc in each of next 2 sts, sk next 3 sts] 12 times, 2 dc in each of next 2 sts, sk next st, sc in next 17 sts; join with sl st in first sc—91 sts.

Fasten off and weave in ends.

CONNECT EYE PIECES

With RS facing you, lay both eye pieces flat next to each other with pointed ends facing out. Find the first dc at the top of each eye piece and count 16 dc toward the center of the eye, put a stitch marker in the 16th dc on each eye piece.

Hold both pieces with WS together, with stitches matching and right eye piece facing toward you. Place a slip knot on the hook.

Joining Row: Working through both thicknesses and beginning in the marked sts, sl st in next 6 sts, working up the nose.

Flatten out the piece.

Notes:

1. There are 85 sts left unworked around each eye piece, for a total of 170 sts all the way around the joined piece.
2. Rnds are now worked all the way around the outer edge of the joined piece.

Rnd 1 (RS): Beginning by working in unworked sts of right eye piece, sc in next st, 2 sc in next st, [sc in next 3 sts, 2 sc in next st] 2 times, sc in next 22 sts (skipping the joining sl st), (hdc, dc, hdc) in next st, sc in next 51 sts, sc2tog (working over last st of right eye piece and first available st of left eye piece), sc in next 51 sts, (hdc, dc, hdc) in next st, sc in next 22 sts (skipping the joining sl st), [2 sc in next st, sc in next 3 sts] 2 times, 2 sc in next st, sl st in next st, ch 1; join with sl st in first sc—179 sts.

Rnd 2: Sk same st as joining sl st, sl st in next 2 sts, [sc in next 4 sts, 2 sc in next st] 2 times, sc in next 16 sts, sc2tog, sc in next 5 sts, (hdc, dc hdc) in next st, [sk next 2 sts, 7 tr in next st, sk next 2 sts, sc in next st] 2 times, sk next st, 5 dc in next st, sk next st, [sc in next 5 sc, 2 sc in next st] 5 times, sc in next 5 sts, sk next 2 sts, 5 tr in next st, sk next 2 sts, sc in next 5 sts, [2 sc in next st, sc in next 5 sts] 5 times, sk next st, 5 dc in next st, sk next st, [sc in next st, sk next 2 sts, 7 tr in next st, sk next 2 sts] 2 times, (hdc, dc, hdc) in next st, sc in next 5 sts, sc2tog, sc in next 16 sts, 2 sc in next st, sc in next 4 sts, 2 sc in next st, sc in next 3 sts, sl st in next st, ch 3, sk last 3 sts; join with sl st in first sc—201 sts.

Rnd 3: Sk same st as joining sl st, sl st in next 3 sts, sc in next 24 sts, sc2tog, sc in next 5 sts, (hdc, dc, hdc) in next st, sc in next 3 sts, [2 sc in each of next 3 sts, sc in next 5 sts] 2 times, 2 sc in next st, sc in next 40 sts, sk next 4 sts, 9 tr in next st, sk next 4 sts, sc in next 40 sts, 2 sc in next st, [sc in next 5 sts, 2 sc in each of next 3 sts] 2 times, sc in next 3 sts, (hdc, dc, hdc) in next st, sc in next 5 sts, sc2tog, sc in next 23 sts, sl st in next st, ch 6, sk last 4 sts; join with sl st in first sc—209 sts.

Fasten off and weave in ends.

OPTIONS

Tie: Sl st in sc between the pair of 7-tr groups on one side of Rnd 2 and chain until you get to a length that fits snug around your head, then sl st in the other sc between the other pair of 7-tr groups.

For a sturdier mask: Buy a plastic masquerade mask at your local craft store. Coat your crocheted mask in fabric stiffener and lay it over the plastic mask. Flatten it over the plastic mask and allow to dry overnight.

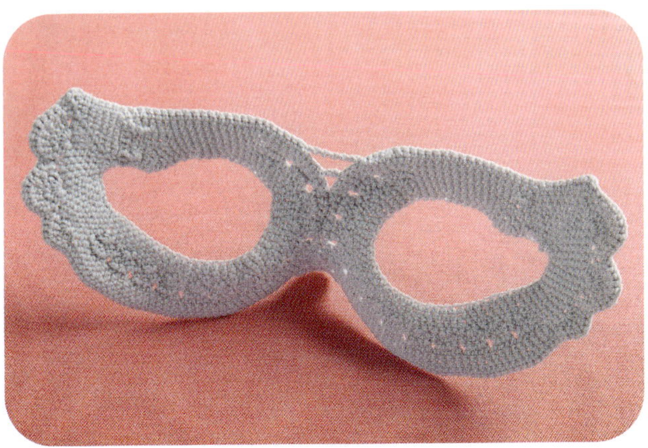

Fae Ear Cuffs

Designed by Sonia Childers of S.Crochet.Designs

No fantasy wardrobe is complete without a touch of fae magic. Slip on these crocheted fae ears and instantly feel the allure of the woodland realms, perfect for a rendezvous under the stars.

Skill Level

Measurements

- Ear Cuffs made with worsted weight yarn (#4 medium): measures approx. 4" (10 cm) long.

Yarn

- Worsted weight yarn (#4 medium) in skin tone color of your choice.
- *Shown:* Big Twist Value (4.3 oz/121 g, 229 yd/246 m, 100% acrylic) in Cream
- Less than 1 skein is required.

Crochet Hook

- 2.75 mm (size C/2). *Note:* This is my preferred hook size, but you may need to use a different size if you are prone to loose or tight tension.

Materials

18-gauge wire, two 11" (28 cm) pieces
General purpose tape

Notions

Scissors
Stitch marker
Tapestry needle

Gauge

Gauge is not critical for this project.

Special Stitch

- **Picot:** Ch 3, sl st in 3rd ch from hook.

CUFFS (MAKE 2)

Make a circle with your wire. Overlap ends by ½" (13 mm) and tape together.

Rnd 1: Place a slip knot on your hook. Insert hook into wire circle, take working yarn over the top of the circle and yarn over, draw a loop back to front of circle (2 loops on hook), take hook over the top of the circle, yarn over and draw through both loops on hook (sc made around the wire), make 59 more sc covering the wire ring; join with sl st in first sc, turn—60 sc.

Flatten the covered wire circle into parallel lines of 30 sc each so that the first st matches the last st, the 2nd st matches the 59th st, the 3rd st matches the 58th st, and so on.

Row 2: Ch 1, working through both layers and beginning by inserting the hook into the first and last st, sc in each pair of sts across, turn—30 sc.

Bend the covered wire into a half heart shape. The working yarn is currently at the bottom of the ear, so curve the top part. The wire can be adjusted later to the shape of your ears.

Scan to watch a video tutorial showing the first two rows and how to form the wire.

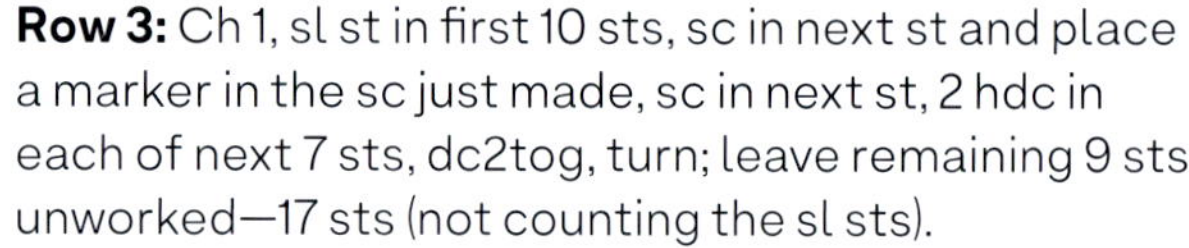

Row 3: Ch 1, sl st in first 10 sts, sc in next st and place a marker in the sc just made, sc in next st, 2 hdc in each of next 7 sts, dc2tog, turn; leave remaining 9 sts unworked—17 sts (not counting the sl sts).

Row 4: Ch 1, dc2tog, hdc2tog, sc in next 8 sts, hdc2tog, dc2tog, turn; leave marked st unworked (do not remove marker)—12 sts.

Row 5: Ch 1, [dc2tog] 2 times, sc in next 4 sts, [dc2tog] 2 times, turn—8 sts.

Row 6: Ch 1, dc2tog, sc in next 4 sts, dc2tog, turn—6 sts.

Row 7: Ch 1, hdc in each st across, turn.

Row 8: Ch 1, sc in next st, hdc in next st, (dc, tr) in next st, ch 1 (for tip of ear), (tr, dc) in next st, hdc in next st, sc in last st—8 sts and 1 ch-1 sp.

Fasten off.

Row 9: Draw up a loop of yarn in marked st so that you are ready to work in ends of rows towards tip of ear, ch 1, work 8 sc evenly spaced in ends of rows along edge, sl st in first 2 sts of Row 8, sc in next 2 sts, (hdc, ch 1, hdc) in ch-1 sp, sc in next 2 sts, sl st in next 2 sts, work 9 sc evenly spaced in ends of rows along edge to Row 4, sc in same st as first st of Row 4, sl st in end of next row, turn—18 sts (counting the sl sts) and 1 ch-1 sp.

With first cuff, work First Ear Row 10.

With second cuff, work Second Ear Row 10.

First Ear

Row 10: Ch 1, working in BLO, sk first st, sl st in next 15 sts, (sc, hdc, picot, sc) in ch-1 sp, sl st in next 13 sts; working in same sts as sl sts of Row 3, work loose sl sts in next 2 sts. The ear will naturally curl, but if your sl sts are too tight, they will curl too much.

Fasten off.

Second Ear

Row 10: Ch 1, working in FLO, sk first st, sl st in next 15 sts, (sc, hdc, picot, sc) in ch-1 sp, sl st in next 13 sts; working in same sts as sl sts of Row 3, work loose sl sts in next 2 sts. The ear will naturally curl, but if your sl sts are too tight, they will curl too much.

Fasten off.

Weave in ends.

Bend the bottom part of each ear cuff to curve around your ear, or curl it outwards and shape it into an S-shape so it places slight pressure on the bottom of the earlobe.

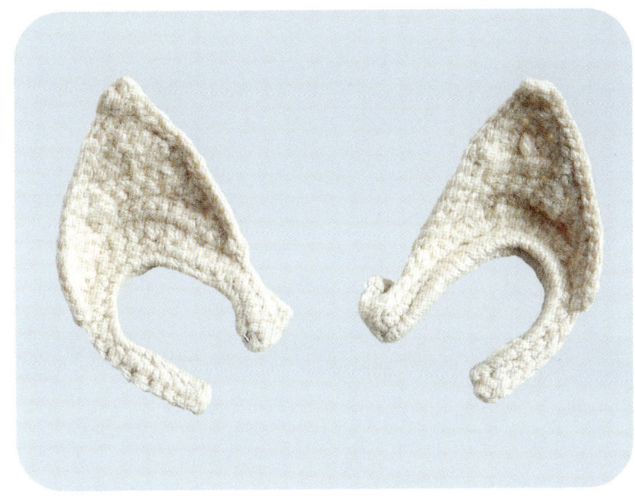

Faun Beanie

Designed by Sonia Childers of S.Crochet.Designs

Are you a misunderstood villain or a brooding antihero? Don't spend hours twisting your hair into complex knots. Embrace your inner dark lord or rebellious queen with this horned beanie.

Skill Level

Measurements

- Beanie made with bulky weight yarn (#5 bulky) and recommended hook size: measures approx. 26" (66 cm) in circumference.

Yarn

- Bulky weight yarn (#5 bulky) in color of your choice.
- *Shown:* I Love This Chunky Yarn (3.5 oz/99 g, 109 yd/100 m, 100% acrylic) in Plumberry (108)
- 2 skeins are required.

Crochet Hook

- 4 mm (size G/6). *Note:* This is my preferred hook size, but you may need to use a different size if you are prone to loose or tight tension.

Notions

Scissors
Stitch markers
Tapestry needle

Gauge

Rnds 1–4 should measure about 4" (10 cm) across from one corner to the opposite corner.

Note

- If you find it difficult to see your stitches, mark the FLO of each ch-1 sp AND the first st of each rnd. (7 stitch markers total). Then, ch 1 and turn. The first marked st (which will be the last ch-1 sp made in the previous rnd) needs to stay there until you come back around because you will be working into that ch-1 sp again to finish the rnd.

BASE

Make a magic ring.

Rnd 1: [Ch 1, hdc in ring] 6 times, ch 1; join with sl st in first hdc, turn—6 hdc and 6 ch-1 sps.

Rnd 2: Ch 1, working in BLO, hdc in first ch-1 sp, [hdc in next st, (hdc, ch 1, hdc) in next ch-1 sp] 5 times, hdc in next st, hdc again in first ch-1 sp, ch 1; join with sl st in first hdc, turn—18 hdc and 6 ch-1 sps.

Rnd 3: Ch 1, working in BLO, hdc in first ch-1 sp, [hdc in next 3 sts, (hdc, ch 1, hdc) in next ch-1 sp] 5 times, hdc in next 3 sts, hdc again in first ch-1 sp, ch 1; join with sl st in first hdc, turn—30 hdc and 6 ch-1 sps.

Rnd 4: Ch 1, working in BLO, hdc in first ch-1 sp, [hdc in next 5 sts, (hdc, ch 1, hdc) in next ch-1 sp] 5 times, hdc in next 5 sts, hdc again in first ch-1 sp, ch 1; join with sl st in first hdc, turn—42 hdc and 6 ch-1 sps.

Note: Check your gauge here. Rnds 1–4 should measure about 4" (10 cm) from one corner across to the opposite corner.

Rnd 5: Ch 1, working in BLO, hdc in first ch-1 sp, [hdc in next 7 sts, (hdc, ch 1, hdc) in next ch-1 sp] 5 times, hdc in next 7 sts, hdc again in first ch-1 sp, ch 1; join with sl st in first hdc, turn—54 hdc and 6 ch-1 sps.

Rnd 6: Ch 1, working in BLO, hdc in first ch-1 sp, [hdc in each st to next ch-1 sp, (hdc, ch 1, hdc) in ch-1 sp] 5 times, hdc in each st to end of rnd, hdc again in first ch-1 sp, ch 1; join with sl st in first hdc, turn—66 hdc and 6 ch-1 sps.

Rnds 7–13: Rep Rnd 6 for 7 more times—150 hdc and 6 ch-1 sps in Rnd 13.

Notes:

1. Place markers in the 1st, 3rd, 4th, and 6th ch-1 sps of Rnd 13.
2. Check your gauge here. Rnds 1–13 should measure about 13" (33 cm) from one corner across to the opposite corner.
3. The piece should be a flat hexagon.

FIRST HORN

Row 1: Ch 1, working in BLO, sc in first (marked) ch-1 sp, hdc in each st to next ch-1 sp, (2 hdc, ch 1, 2 hdc) in ch-1 sp, hdc in each st to next (marked) ch-1 sp, sc in ch-1 sp, turn; leave remaining sts unworked—56 sts and 1 ch-1 sp.

Row 2: Ch 1, working in BLO, sc in first marked ch-1 sp, hdc in each st to next ch-1 sp, (2 hdc, ch 1, 2 hdc) in ch-1 sp, hdc in each st to last st, sc in last st, turn—60 sts and 1 ch-1 sp.

Rows 3 and 4: Rep Row 2 twice—68 sts and 1 ch-1 sp in Row 4.

Row 5 (Seam Horn): Fold last row in half, bringing first st of row BEHIND last st of row; working through both thicknesses, sc in each of the 34 sc pairs across.

Fasten off.

SECOND HORN

Skip the next (unmarked) ch-1 sp following Row 1 of the first horn, draw up a loop in the next (marked) ch-1 sp.

Rep Rows 1–5 of first horn.

BAND

With the horns toward you, draw up a loop in the st following the last marked ch-1 sp. Remove stitch markers.

Rnd 1: Ch 1, working in BLO, sc in same st as joining, sc in next 24 sts; sc in end of each of next 8 horn rows; working in BLO, sc in next 25 sts, sc in end of each of next 8 horn rows; join with sl st in first sc, turn—66 sc.

Rnds 2–4: Ch 1, working in BLO, hdc in each st around; join with sl st in first hdc, turn—66 hdc.

Weave in end.

Turn your Beanie inside out, grab the end tails from the horns, bring them outside of the Beanie and pull on them to help point the horns.

Weave in any remaining tails.

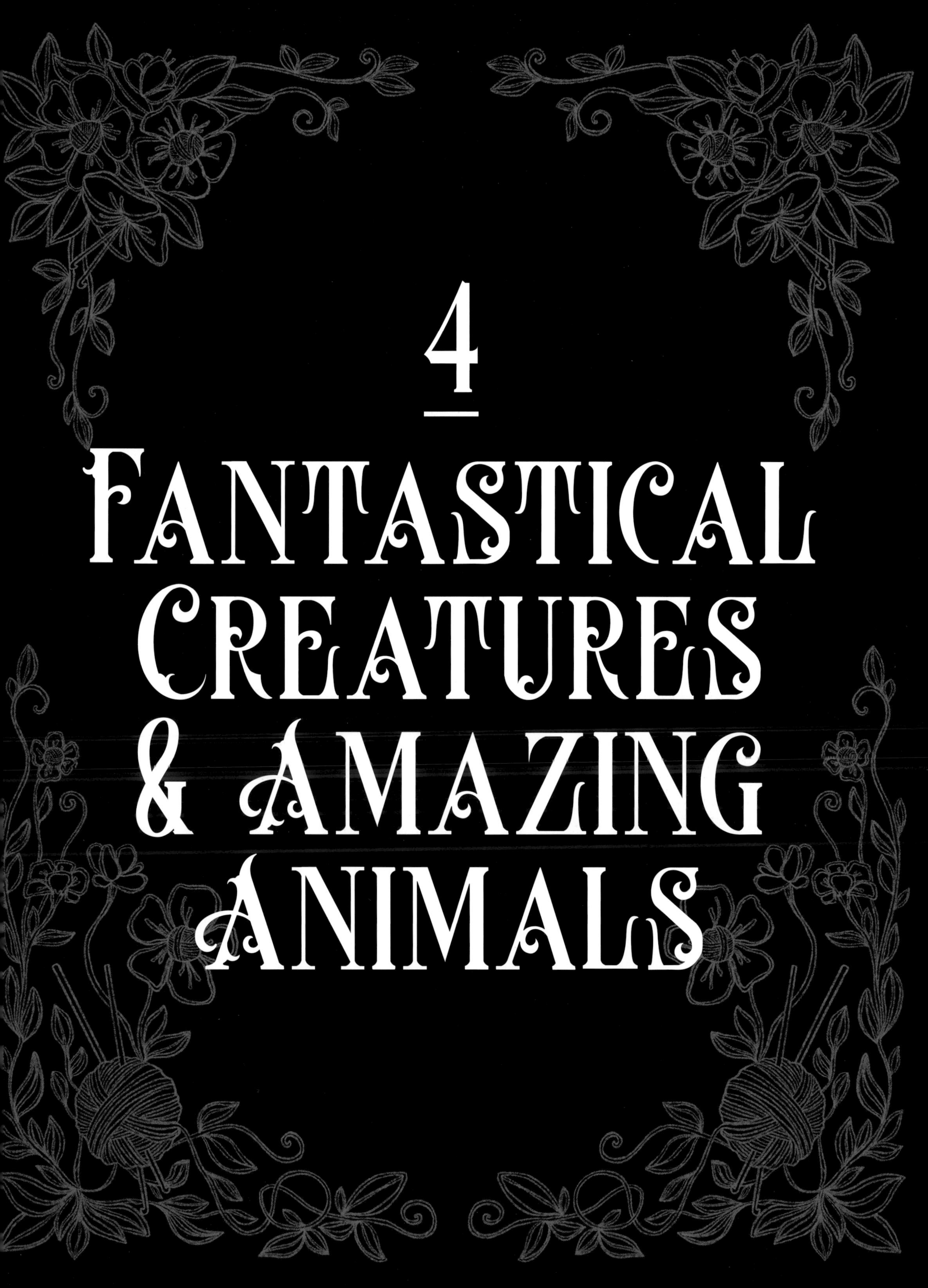

4

Fantastical Creatures & Amazing Animals

Dark Siren

Designed by Daniella Flete of Daniella's Workshop

Beware the call of the deep. With this dark siren creation, you'll lure even the most cautious sailors into the abyss. There's no escape from the deadly allure of your craft, where each stitch seals their fate with a spell as irresistible as the pull of the sea. Your power to crochet? The only thing stronger than the tide.

Skill Level

Measurements

- Siren made with worsted weight yarn (#4 medium): measures approx. 12" (30.5 cm) tall.

Yarn

- Worsted weight yarn (#4 medium) in blue, gray, and black.
- *Shown:* I Love This Yarn (7 oz/198 g, 355 yd/324 m, 100% acrylic) in Light Gray (190) and Black (30)
- I Love This Yarn Metallic (5 oz/142 g, 252 yd/230 m, 97% acrylic, 3% metallic polyester) in Teal Sparkle (766)
- Less than 1 skein of each color is required for each piece.

Crochet Hook

- 2.75 mm (size C/2). *Note:* This is my preferred hook size, but you may need to use different sizes if you are prone to loose or tight tension.

Materials

Stuffing
18-gauge wire (optional)
12 mm black safety eyes

Notions

Scissors
Stitch markers
Tapestry needle
Wire cutters

Gauge

Gauge is not critical for this project.

TAIL

With blue yarn, make a magic ring.

Rnd 1: Work 4 sc into ring; do not join, work in continuous rnds (spiral).

Place a marker in last st made to indicate end of rnd. Move marker up as each rnd is completed.

Rnds 2 and 3: Sc in each st around (2 rnds).

Rnd 4: 2 sc in next st, sc in next 3 sts—5 sts.

Rnds 5 and 6: Sc in each st around (2 rnds).

Rnd 7: 2 sc in next st, sc in next 4 sts—6 sts.

Rnds 8–15: Sc in each st around (8 rnds).

Rnd 16: [Sc in next 2 sts, 2 sc in next st] 2 times—8 sts.

Begin stuffing and continue as you go.

If you want the body to be posable, cut a 24" (61 cm) piece of wire, fold it in half, and put the folded loop in the end of the tail. Continue working around the wire.

Rnd 17: 2 sc in next st, sc in next 7 sts—9 sts.

Rnd 18: Sc in each st around.

Rnd 19: Sc in next 4 sts, 2 sc in next st, sc in next 4 sts—10 sts.

Rnd 20: Sc in each st around.

Rnd 21: 2 sc in next st, sc in next 9 sts—11 sts.

Rnd 22: Sc in each st around.

Rnd 23: Sc in next 5 sts, 2 sc in next st, sc in next 5 sts—12 sts.

Rnd 24: Sc in each st around.

Rnd 25: [Sc in next 5 sts, 2 sc in next st] 2 times—14 sts.

Rnd 26: Sc in next 3 sts, 2 sc in next st, sc in next 6 sts, 2 sc in next st, sc in next 3 sts—16 sts.

Rnd 27: [Sc in next 7 sts, 2 sc in next st] 2 times—18 sts.

Rnd 28: [Sc in next 5 sts, 2 sc in next st] 3 times—21 sts.

Rnd 29: Sc in next 3 sts, [2 sc in next st, sc in next 6 sts] 2 times, 2 sc in next st, sc in next 3 sts—24 sts.

Rnd 30: [Sc in next 7 sts, 2 sc in next st] 3 times—27 sts.

Rnds 31 and 32: Sc in each st around (2 rnds).

BODY

Note: In Rnds 34–38, whenever light gray yarn (body color) is worked into a blue st (tail color), work in BLO.

Rnd 34: With blue, sc in next 10 sts; with light gray, sc in next 3 sts; with blue, sc in next 14 sts—27 sts.

Rnd 35: With blue, sc in next 8 sts; with light gray, sc in next 7 sts; with blue, sc in next 12 sts—27 sts.

Rnd 36: With blue, sc in next 3 sts, sc2tog, sc in next 2 sts; with light gray, sc in next 4 sts, sc2tog, sc in next 3 sts; with blue, sc in next 4 sts, sc2tog, sc in next 5 sts—24 sts.

Rnd 37: With blue, sc in next 5 sts; with light gray, sc in next 10 sts; with blue, sc in next 9 sts—24 sts.

Change to light gray yarn. Fasten off blue yarn.

Rnd 38: Sc in each st around.

Rnd 39: Sc in next 2 sts, [sc2tog] 3 times, sc in next 6 sts, [sc2tog] 3 times, sc in next 4 sts—18 sts.

Rnd 40: Sc in each st around.

Rnd 41: Sc in next 3 sts, 2 sc in next st, sc in next 8 sts, 2 sc in next st, sc in next 5 sts—20 sts.

Rnd 42: Sc in each st around.

Rnd 43: Sc in next 4 sts, 2 sc in next st, sc in next 9 sts, 2 sc in next st, sc in next 5 sts—22 sts.

Rnd 44: Sc in each st around.

Rnd 45: Sc in next 5 sts, 2 sc in next st, sc in next 10 sts, 2 sc in next st, sc in next 5 sts—24 sts.

Rnd 46: Sc in next 8 sts, 2 dc in each of next 3 sts, sc in next 2 sts, 2 dc in each of next 3 sts, sc in next 8 sts—30 sts. *Optional:* Change to blue (tail color) for the dc sts for a shell bra.

Rnd 47: Sc in each st around. *Optional:* Change to blue (tail color) for the 6 sts on top of the dc sts to continue shell bra.

Rnd 48: Sc in next 8 sts, [sc2tog] 3 times, sc in next 2 sts, [sc2tog] 3 times, sc in next 8 sts—24 sts.

Rnds 49 and 50: Sc in each st around (2 rnds).

Rnd 51: Sc in next 4 sts, [sc2tog] 3 times, sc in next 6 sts, [sc2tog] 3 times, sc in next 2 sts—18 sts.

Rnd 52: [Sc2tog] 9 times—9 sts.

Rnds 53 and 54: Sc in each st around (2 rnds).

Make sure the body and neck are fully stuffed.

Rnd 55: Working in FLO, 2 sc in each of next 9 sts—18 sts.

Rnd 56: [Sc in next 2 sts, 2 sc in next st] 6 times—24 sts.

Rnds 57–62: Sc in each st around (6 rnds),

Insert safety eyes between Rnds 60 and 61, 4 sts apart.

Make sure neck is stuffed firmly and continue stuffing the head as you close the head.

Rnd 63: [Sc in next 2 sts, sc2tog] 6 times—18 sts.

Rnd 64: [sc in next st, sc2tog] 6 times—12 sts.

Rnd 65: [Sc2tog] 6 times—6 sts.

Fasten off, leaving a long tail. Thread tail through sts of last rnd and pull to close opening. Weave in end securely.

ARMS (MAKE 2)

With light gray yarn, make a magic ring.

Rnd 1: Work 6 sc into ring; do not join, work in continuous rnds (spiral).

Place a marker in last st made to indicate end of rnd. Move marker up as each rnd is completed.

Rnds 2–7: Sc in each st around (6 rnds).

Rnd 8: Sc2tog, sc in next 4 sts—5 sts.

Rnds 9–12: Sc in each st around (4 rnds).

Rnd 13: Sc2tog, sc in next 3 sts—4 sts.

Rnds 14 and 15: Sc in each st around (2 rnds).

Rnd 16: [2 sc in next st, sc in next st] 2 times—6 sts.

Rnd 17: Sc in each st around.

Flatten Rnd 17 so that there are 3 sts along each side.

Row 18: Working through both thicknesses, sc in next 3 sts, turn.

Row 19: Ch 1, sc3tog—1 st.

Fasten off and hide loose end.

TAIL FANS (MAKE 2)

Foundation Chain: With blue yarn, ch 6.

First Strand: Sl st in 2nd ch from hook; ch 18, sl st in 2nd ch from hook and in next 15 ch (leave last ch unworked), sl st in next ch of foundation ch; do not fasten off, continue with instructions for next strand.

Second Strand: Ch 15, sl st in 2nd ch from hook and in next 12 ch (leave last ch unworked), sl st in next ch of foundation ch.

Third Strand: Ch 12, sl st in 2nd ch from hook and in next 9 ch (leave last ch unworked), sl st in next ch of foundation ch.

Fourth Strand: Ch 9, sl st in 2nd ch from hook and in next 6 ch (leave last ch unworked), sl st in next ch of foundation ch.

Fifth Strand: Ch 6, sl st in 2nd ch from hook and in next 3 ch (leave last ch unworked), sl st in next ch of foundation ch.

Fasten off, leaving a long tail for sewing.

EARS (MAKE 2)

With light gray yarn, leaving a long beginning tail, ch 3.

Row 1: Sc in 2nd ch from hook and in next ch, turn—2 sts.

Row 2: Ch 1, sc2tog, turn—1 st.

Row 3: Ch 1, sc in st.

Fasten off and weave in ending tail.

ASSEMBLY

Nose: With a strand of light gray yarn, embroider a straight stitch nose, passing over one stitch between Rnds 58 and 59, centered between the eyes.

Eyebrows and Lashes: With a strand of black yarn, embroider slanted eyebrows above the eyes. Position is personal preference. Continue with the strand of black yarn and line the top of the eyes to create lashes. Secure yarn and hide loose ends.

Ears: Sew ears on the side of the head approx. 2 sts behind the eyes. Place the bottom of the ears between Rnds 57 and 58 and the top of the ears between Rnds 60 and 61.

Tail Fans: Attach tail fans on opposite sides of the tail between Rnds 1 and 5 of the tail. The longer strands of the tail fans should be at Rnd 5, and the short strands should be attached at the magic ring.

Arms: Cut a long strand of light gray yarn and sew the arms onto the sides of the body, with the top of the arms at Rnd 50 of the body. *Optional:* If you'd like the arms to be posable, cut a piece of wire approx. 7" (18 cm) long. Pass the wire through the side of the body between Rnds 48 and 49. With an equal amount of wire on both sides, insert the wire into the arms between Rnds 2 and 3, and bend the wire at the "armpit" to let the arms lay flat against the sides. When using wire, only pass a couple sewing stitches around the wire to secure the arms to the body. This allows maximum arm movement.

HAIR

With black yarn, cut approx. 36 strands of yarn about 14" (35.5 cm) long. Cut one more strand of black yarn about 24" (61 cm) long for working yarn. Thread the working yarn onto tapestry needle and insert it in the back of the head and out through the forehead area where you would like the hair line to start.

Bunch together four of the 14" (35.5 cm) strands and sew a loop with your working yarn over the strands to secure them in place. Bring working yarn out in the next st back from the hair strands and then repeat this process with another bunch of 4 strands until all 36 strands have been used and the hair falls neatly all the way to the back of the head.

Bring working yarn back out in the same place as you started in the back of the head, tie a knot with the two tails, and hide them inside the head.

Give the doll a haircut to even out the length of the hair and then style the hair. I like to pull the front several strands back behind the ear on one side, leaving a few strands in front of the ear.

Mysterious Fae Warrior

Designed by Amanda Sennett of Crochet By A Manda Lorian

The enigmatic fae warrior—guardian of realms, protector of the innocent, and sometimes the one who falls for the human they swore to defend. Though our heroine can fight her own battles, why not let the 6-foot-something, combat-trained fae warrior do the heavy lifting? After all, his greatest drive is to protect not just his cadre and his family but also his one true mate.

Skill Level

Measurements

- Doll made with worsted weight yarn (#4 medium): measures approx. 9" (23 cm) tall.

Yarn

- Worsted weight yarn (#4 medium) in light tan, black, navy blue, light gray, and dark gray.
- *Shown:* Big Twist Value (4.3 oz/121 g, 229 yd/246 m, 100% acrylic) in Cream
- I Love This Yarn (7 oz/198 g, 355 yd/324 m, 100% acrylic) in Black (30), Navy Blue (90), Light Gray (190), Grey Beard (201), and Gray Mist (200)
- Less than 1 skein of each color is required.
- *See page 97 for yarn information on the Woodland Fae Warrior.*

Crochet Hook

- 2.75 mm (size C/2). *Note:* This is my preferred hook size, but you may need to use a different size if you are prone to loose or tight tension.

Materials

Stuffing
15 mm black safety eyes. I like to have flat eyes and have found them at www.glasseyesonline.com.

Notions

Scissors
Stitch markers
Tapestry needle

Gauge

Gauge is not critical for this project.

Note

- If you want to add some extra flair to your warrior, follow the bookmark pattern for the bat or angel wings (found on page 9) and sew them onto his back after assembly.

HEAD

With light tan yarn, make a magic ring.

Rnd 1: Work 8 sc into ring; do not join, work in continuous rnds (spiral).

Place a marker in last st made to indicate end of rnd. Move marker up as each rnd is completed.

Rnd 2: 2 sc in each of next 8 sts—16 sts.

Rnd 3: [2 sc in each of next 2 sts, sc in next 2 sts] 4 times—24 sts.

Rnd 4: Sc in next st, 2 sc in each of next 2 sts, [sc in next 4 sts, 2 sc in each of next 2 sts] 3 times, sc in last 3 sts—32 sts.

Rnd 5: Sc in next 2 sts, 2 sc in each of next 2 sts, [sc in next 6 sts, 2 sc in each of next 2 sts] 3 times, sc in last 4 sts—40 sts.

Rnd 6: Sc in next 3 sts, 2 sc in each of next 2 sts, [sc in next 8 sts, 2 sc in each of next 2 sts] 3 times, sc in last 5 sts—48 sts.

Rnds 7–17: Sc in each st around (11 rnds).

Notes:

- If you are using safety eyes, insert them now between Rnds 12 and 13 approx. 6 sts apart.
- If needed, move the end of rnd marker over a space or two so that the 2 decreases in the next rounds line up with the 2 increases in Rnds 3–6.

Rnd 18: Sc in next 5 sts, [sc2tog] 2 times, *sc in next 8 sts, [sc2tog] 2 times; rep from * to last 3 sts, sc in last 3 sts—40 sts.

Rnd 19: Sc in next 4 sts, [sc2tog] 2 times, *sc in next 6 sts, [sc2tog] 2 times; rep from * to last 2 sts, sc in last 2 sts—32 sts.

Stuff the head, focusing on the corners to make sure the head stays in a cube shape.

Rnd 20: Sc in next 3 sts, [sc2tog] 2 times, *sc in next 4 sts, [sc2tog] 2 times; rep from * to last st, sc in last st—24 sts.

Rnd 21: *[Sc2tog] 2 times, sc in next 2 sts; rep from * around—16 sts.

Rnd 22: [Sc in next 2 sts, sc2tog] 4 times—12 sts.

Rnd 23: Sc in each st around.

Fasten off, leaving a long tail for sewing the neck to the body.

NOSE

With a strand of light tan yarn, embroider a straight stitch nose, passing the strand over 3 or 4 sts between Rnds 14 and 15, centered between the eyes.

EYEBROWS

With a long strand of black yarn, embroider straight stitch eyebrows just above the eyes.

EARS

With light tan yarn, make a magic ring.

Row 1: Work 6 sc into ring, turn.

Row 2: Ch 1, sc in next 3 sts; leave last 3 sts unworked, turn—3 sts.

Row 3: Ch 1, sc in each st across, turn.

Row 4: Do not ch, sk first st, sc in last 2 sts, turn—2 sts.

Row 5: Do not ch, sk first st, sc in last st, turn—1 st.

Row 6: Ch 1, sc in st.

Fasten off, leaving a long tail for sewing.

Sew ears to head, about 4 sts back from the eyes, with the bottom of the ears in line with the nose and the top points in line with the top of the eyes.

ARMS (MAKE 2)

With light tan yarn, make a magic ring.

Rnd 1: Work 7 sc into ring; do not join, work in continuous rnds (spiral).

Place a marker in last st made to indicate end of rnd. Move marker up as each rnd is completed.

Rnd 2: Sc in each st around.

Change to navy blue.

Rnd 3: Working in BLO, sl st in each st around.

Rnd 4: Working in BLO, sc in each st around.

Rnds 5–12: Sc in each st around (8 rnds).

No need to stuff arms.

Flatten top of arm. Working through both thicknesses, work 3 sc evenly spaced across top.

Fasten off. Set aside for now. Arms will be crocheted in place when making body.

LEGS (MAKE 2)

With black yarn, make a magic ring.

Rnd 1: Work 6 sc into ring; do not join, work in continuous rnds (spiral).

Place a marker in last st made to indicate end of rnd. Move marker up as each rnd is completed.

Rnd 2: 2 sc in each of next 6 sts—12 sts.

Rnd 3: [Sc in next st, 2 sc in next st] 6 times—18 sts.

Rnd 4: Working in BLO, sc in each st around.

Note: At this point you may have a cone shape, but that's okay. We'll be pushing that up into the foot during stuffing to create a solid base.

Rnd 5: Sc in each st around.

Rnd 6: Sc in next 3 sts, [sc2tog] 6 times, sc in last 3 sts—12 sts.

Rnds 7–10: Sc in each st around (4 rnds).

Start stuffing around the outside edges of the foot. Keep the bottom pushed up into the foot if it's cone-shaped and stuff around it. Continue stuffing the leg as you go.

Change to navy blue.

Rnd 11: Keeping sts loose and working in BLO, sl st in each st around.

Rnd 12: Working in BLO, sc in each st around.

Rnds 13–17: Sc in each st around (5 rnds).

Fasten off first leg.

Work additional sc in each st until you reach the inner middle of the leg (I had to work sc in next 5 sts).

Do not fasten off second leg.

JOIN LEGS

Rnd 18: Hold legs together, with feet facing in the same direction and making sure both legs have the color change centered in the back, sc in each st of first leg then sc in each st of second leg—24 sts.

Rnds 19–21: Sc in each st around (3 rnds).

Do not fasten off.

BODY

Change to black yarn.

Rnd 22: Working in BLO, sl st in each st around.

Rnd 23: Working in BLO, sc in each st around.

Rnds 24–30: Sc in each st around (7 rnds).

Begin stuffing body and continue stuffing until piece is complete.

JOIN ARMS TO BODY

Rnd 31: Sc in next 7 sts of body only, sc in next 3 sts through first arm and body, sc in next 8 sts of body only, sc in next 3 sts through second arm and body, sc in next 3 sts of body only—24 sts.

Rnd 32: [Sc2tog] 12 times—12 sts.

Change to light tan yarn.

Rnd 33: Working in BLO, sl st in each st around.

Rnd 34: Working in BLO, [sc in next 2 sts, sc2tog] 3 times—9 sts.

Rnds 35–39: Sc in each st around (5 rnds).

Make sure the neck is stuffed firmly so it will support the head.

Rnd 40: [Sc in next st, sc2tog] 3 times—6 sts.

Fasten off, leaving a long tail for sewing.

BELT

With dark gray yarn, ch 14.

Fasten off. Wrap belt around shirt/pant color change. Secure in the back.

SWORD

With light gray yarn, ch 15.

Row 1: Sl st in 2nd ch from hook, sc in remaining 13 ch, turn—13 sts (not including sl st).

Change to black yarn.

Row 2: Ch 3, sc in 2nd ch from hook and in next ch, work 2 sc into end of Row 1, turn—4 sts.

Row 3: Ch 2, sc in 2nd ch from hook, sc in next 2 sts; leave remaining 2 sts unworked, turn—3 sts.

Row 4: Ch 1, sc in next st; leave remaining 2 sts unworked, turn—1 st.

Rows 5 and 6: Ch 1, sc in st, turn.

Fasten off.

Weave in ends. Place sword snuggly under the belt.

CLOAK

With light gray yarn, leaving a long beginning tail for sewing, ch 23

Row 1: Dc in 2nd ch from hook and in next 5 ch, hdc in next 8 ch, sc in next 8 ch, turn—22 sts.

Row 2: Ch 1, sc in next 8 sts, hdc in next 8 sts, dc in next 6 sts, turn.

Row 3: Ch 2, dc in first 6 sts, hdc in next 8 sts, sc in next 8 sts, turn.

Rows 4–13: Rep Rows 2 and 4 (additional rows can be worked if you would like the cloak to be wider).

Fasten off.

With beginning and ending tails, sew the cloak just behind both shoulders.

SHOULDER SHIELD (MAKE 2)

With dark gray yarn, ch 7.

Row 1: Sc in 2nd ch from hook and in next 5 ch, turn—6 sts.

Row 2: Do not ch, sk first st, sc in next 3 sts, sc2tog, turn—4 sts.

Row 3: Do not ch, sk first st, sc in next st, sc2tog, ch, turn—2 sts.

Row 4: Ch 1, sc in each st across.

Fasten off, leaving a long tail. Weave long tail to corner of beginning edge, opposite beginning tail.

Sew the top corners of the shoulder shields over the top of the arms. The back of the shields should slightly cover where the cloak is sewn onto the body.

ATTACH HEAD TO BODY

Thread the long tail on the neck through the hole in the bottom of the head and out through the top of the head. Pull that tail while smashing the head down on the neck as far as it will go. The head should sit almost on the shoulders. Feed the tail back down through the head and out at the neck. Make sure the head is facing forward before sewing. Using the tail from the bottom of the head, sew around the base of the head and neck to secure the head in place. Tie the two tails together to secure and hide them inside the head.

HAIR

With black yarn, cut approx. 48 strands of yarn about 12" (30.5 cm) long.

Cut one more strand of black yarn about 24" (61 cm) long, for working yarn. Thread the working yarn onto tapestry needle and insert it in the back of the head and out through the forehead area where you would like the hairline to start.

Bunch together four of the 12" (30.5 cm) strands and sew a loop with your working yarn over the strands to secure them in place. Bring working yarn out in the next st back from the hair strands and then repeat this process with another bunch of four strands until all 48 have been used and the hair falls neatly all the way to the back of the head.

Bring working yarn back out in the same place as you started in the back of the head, tie a knot with the two tails, and hide them inside the head.

Give the doll a haircut to even out the length of the hair and then style the hair. I like to pull the front several strands back behind the ear, leaving a few strands in front of the ears.

Now your Fae Warrior is ready for his fight! He will protect your bookshelf with everything he has!

Scan to watch a video tutorial showing the hair assembly.

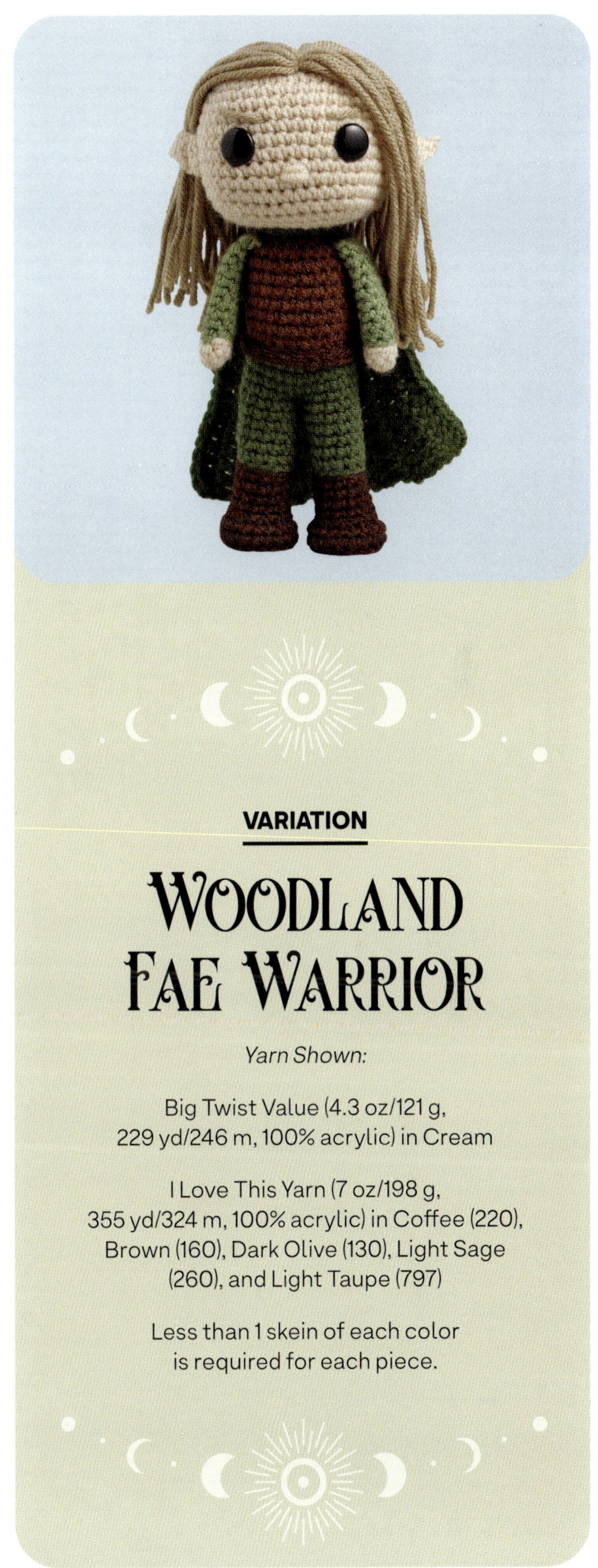

VARIATION

WOODLAND FAE WARRIOR

Yarn Shown:

Big Twist Value (4.3 oz/121 g, 229 yd/246 m, 100% acrylic) in Cream

I Love This Yarn (7 oz/198 g, 355 yd/324 m, 100% acrylic) in Coffee (220), Brown (160), Dark Olive (130), Light Sage (260), and Light Taupe (797)

Less than 1 skein of each color is required for each piece.

Wise Raven

Designed by Amanda Sennett of Crochet By A Manda Lorian

Channel the wisdom of the majestic raven as it guides your hero—or you—through prophecies, quests, and inevitable romance. Whether you're searching for answers or your fated mate, this wise bird is always one step ahead.

Skill Level

Measurements

- Raven made with worsted weight yarn (#4 medium): measures approx. 12" (30.5 cm) tall.

Yarn

- Worsted weight yarn (#4 medium) in gray and black.
- *Shown:* I Love This Yarn (7 oz/198 g, 355 yd/324 m, 100% acrylic) in Grey Beard (201) and Black (30)
- Less than 1 skein of each color is required for each piece.

Crochet Hook

- 2.75 mm (size C/2). *Note:* This is my preferred hook size, but you may need to use different sizes if you are prone to loose or tight tension.

Materials

Stuffing
18-gauge wire
12 mm black safety eyes

Notions

Scissors
Stitch markers
Tapestry needle
Wire cutters

Gauge

Gauge is not critical for this project.

Special Stitch

- **htr:** Yarn over two times, insert hook into stitch, pull up a loop, yarn over and pull through two loops, yarn over and pull through the three remaining loops.

BEAK

Top of Beak

With gray yarn, ch 2.

Row 1: Sc in 2nd ch from hook, turn—1 st.

Row 2: Ch 1, 2 sc in next st, turn—2 sts.

Row 3: Ch 1, 2 sc in each of next 2 sts, turn—4 sts.

Row 4: Ch 1, 2 sc in next st, sc in next 2 sts, 2 sc in next st, turn—6 sts.

Rows 5–10: Ch 1, sc in each st across, turn (6 rows).

Row 11: Ch 1, sc in each st across, do not turn.

Edging: Working in ends of rows, sc evenly along the side edge of piece, 3 sc in tip, work the same number (as along first side edge) of sc evenly spaced along other side.

Fasten off.

Bottom of Beak

With gray yarn, make a magic ring.

Rnd 1: Work 4 sc into ring; do not join, work in continuous rnds (spiral).

Place a marker in last st made to indicate end of rnd. Move marker up as each rnd is completed.

Rnd 2: [Sc in next st, 2 sc in next st] 2 times—6 sts.

Rnd 3: [Sc in next st, 2 sc in next st] 3 times—9 sts.

Rnds 4–11: Sc in each st around (8 rnds).

Rnd 12: Place top beak on top of bottom beak, with 6 sts of last row of top beak matching first 6 sts of last rnd of bottom beak; working through both thicknesses, [sc in next 2 sts, 2 sc in next st] 2 times; working in bottom beak only, sc in next 2 sts, 2 sc in next st—12 sts.

HEAD

Change to black yarn.

Rnd 13: [Sc in next st, 2 sc in next st] 6 times—18 sts.

Rnd 14: Working in BLO, [sc in next 2 sts, 2 sc in next st] 6 times—24 sts.

Rnd 15: [Sc in next 3 sts, 2 sc in next st] 6 times—30 sts.

Rnd 16: [Sc in next 4 sts, 2 sc in next st] 6 times—36 sts.

Rnds 17–22: Sc in each st around (6 rnds).

Insert safety eyes between Rnds 15 and 16, about 11 or 12 sts apart. Make sure the eyes are centered over the beak.

Begin stuffing lightly in the beak and continue to stuff the head moderately until closed.

Rnd 23: [Sc in next 4 sts, sc2tog] 6 times—30 sts.

Rnd 24: Sc in each st around.

Rnd 25: [Sc in next 3 sts, sc2tog] 6 times—24 sts.

Rnd 26: Sc in each st around.

Rnd 27: [Sc in next 2 sts, sc2tog] 6 times—18 sts.

Rnd 28: [Sc in next st, sc2tog] 6 times—12 sts.

Rnd 29: [Sc2tog] 6 times—6 sts.

Fasten off, leaving a long tail. With tail, sew the hole closed. Hido loose end inside the head.

Next rnd: Return to the free front loops left from Rnd 14. Attach a new strand of black yarn and work a sc in each loop around—18 sts.

Next rnd: Sc in each st around.

Fasten off and hide tail inside head.

BODY

With black yarn, ch 6.

Rnd 1: Sc in 2nd ch from hook and in next 3 ch, 3 sc in last ch; working along opposite side of foundation ch, sc in next 3 ch, 2 sc in last ch; do not join, work in continuous rnds (spiral)—12 sts.

Place a marker in last st made to indicate end of rnd. Move marker up as each rnd is completed.

Rnd 2: [Sc in next st, 2 sc in next st] 6 times—18 sts.

Rnds 3–9: Sc in each st around (7 rnds).

Rnd 10: Sc in next st, [2 sc in next st, sc in next 2 sts] 2 times, 2 sc in next st, sc in last 10 sts—21 sts.

Rnd 11: Sc in next 2 sts, [2 sc in next st, sc in next 3 sts] 2 times, 2 sc in next st, sc in last 10 sts—24 sts.

Rnd 12: Sc in next 3 sts, [2 sc in next st, sc in next 4 sts] 2 times, 2 sc in next st, sc in last 10 sts—27 sts.

Rnd 13: Sc in next 4 sts, [2 sc in next st, sc in next 5 sts] 2 times, 2 sc in next st, sc in last 10 sts—30 sts.

Rnd 14: Sc in next 5 sts, [2 sc in next st, sc in next 6 sts] 2 times, 2 sc in next st, sc in last 10 sts—33 sts.

Rnd 15: Sc in next 6 sts, [2 sc in next st, sc in next 7 sts] 2 times, 2 sc in next st, sc in last 10 sts—36 sts.

Rnd 16: Sc in next 6 sts, [2 sc in next st, sc in next 8 sts] 2 times, 2 sc in next st, sc in last 11 sts—39 sts.

Rnd 17: Sc in next 7 sts, [2 sc in next st, sc in next 9 sts] 2 times, 2 sc in next st, sc in last 11 sts—42 sts.

Rnd 18: Sc in next 8 sts, [2 sc in next st, sc in next 10 sts] 2 times, 2 sc in next st, sc in last 11 sts—45 sts.

Rnds 19–28: Sc in each st around (10 rnds).

Begin stuffing and continue until completed.

Rnd 29: [Sc in next 13 sts, sc2tog] 3 times—42 sts.

Rnds 30–32: Sc in each st around (3 rnds).

Rnd 33: [Sc in next 12 sts, sc2tog] 3 times—39 sts.

Rnds 34–36: Sc in each st around (3 rnds).

Rnd 37: [Sc in next 11 sts, sc2tog] 3 times—36 sts.

Rnds 38 and 39: Sc in each st around (2 rnds).

Rnd 40: [Sc in next 10 sts, sc2tog] 3 times—33 sts.

Rnds 41 and 42: Sc in each st around (2 rnds).

Rnd 43: [Sc in next 9 sts, sc2tog] 3 times—30 sts.

Rnd 44: Sc in each st around.

Fasten off, leaving a long tail for sewing. With tail, sew head to body.

LEG BUMPS (MAKE 2)

With black yarn, make a magic ring.

Rnd 1: Work 6 sc into ring; do not join, work in continuous rnds (spiral).

Place a marker in last st made to indicate end of rnd. Move marker up as each rnd is completed.

Rnd 2: 2 sc in each of next 6 sts—12 sts.

Rnd 3: [Sc in next 3 sts, 2 sc in next st] 3 times—15 sts.

Rnd 4: [Sc in next 4 sts, 2 sc in next st] 3 times, turn—18 sts.

Row 5: Ch 1, sc in next 9 sts; leave remaining 9 sts unworked, turn.

Row 6: Ch 1, sc in next 9 sts, sc in each of the 9 unworked sts from the previous rnd; sl st in first st of this row—18 sts.

Fasten off, leaving a long tail for sewing leg bumps onto the body. With tail, sew leg bumps to bottom of body. Add a little bit of stuffing as you sew.

TAIL FEATHERS (MAKE 3)

With black yarn, ch 21.

Rnd 1: Sc in 2nd ch from hook and in next 18 ch, 3 sc in last ch; working along opposite side of foundation ch, sc in next 18 ch, 2 sc in last ch; work in continuous rnds (spiral)—42 sts.

Place a marker in last st made to indicate end of rnd. Move marker up as each rnd is completed.

Rnd 2: 2 sc in next st, sc in next 18 sts, 2 hdc in each of next 3 sts, sc in next 18 sts, 2 sc in each of next 2 sts—48 sts.

Fasten off, leaving a long tail for sewing. Hide beginning tail. Sew tail feathers onto the back of the body, a few rows above the starting bump of the body. Sew two feathers side by side and sew the third over the top of the first two.

WINGS (MAKE 2)

Wing Top

With black yarn, make a magic ring.

Row 1: Work 5 sc into ring, turn—5 sts.

Row 2: Ch 1, 2 sc in each of next 5 sts, turn—10 sts.

Row 3: Ch 1, sc in each st across, turn.

Row 4: Ch 1, [sc in next st, 2 sc in next st] 5 times, turn—15 sts.

Row 5: Ch 1, sc in each st across, do not turn—15 sts.

Row 6: Ch 1, working in ends of rows, work 4 sc, 4 hdc, and 3 dc evenly spaced along straight edge, turn—11 sts.

Row 7: Ch 3, 2 tr in first st, 2 htr in next st, 2 dc in each of next 2 sts, 2 hdc in each of next 2 sts, 2 sc in each of next 2 sts, sc in next 3 sts, do not turn—19 sts.

Fasten off, leaving a long tail for sewing wing to body later.

Wing Feathers

Attach a new strand of black yarn in the 2nd st of Row 7 of wing top.

Row 1: Ch 6, sc in 2nd ch from hook, sc in next 4 ch, sl st in next st of wing top, turn—5 sts (not including the sl st).

From this point on, work all stitches in BLO (except sl sts worked into the wing top).

Row 2: Ch 1, sk sl st, sc in next 5 sts, turn.

Row 3: Ch 1, sc in next 5 sts, sl st in next st of wing top, turn.

Row 4: Ch 1, sk sl st, sc in next 5 sts, turn.

Row 5: Ch 4, sc in 2nd ch from hook and in next 2 ch, sc in next 5 sts, sl st in next st of wing top, turn—8 sts (not including the sl st).

Row 6: Ch 1, sk sl st, sc in next 8 sts, turn.

Row 7: Ch 1, sc in next 8 sts, sl st in next st of wing top, turn.

Row 8: Ch 1, sk sl st, sc in next 8 sts, turn.

Row 9: Ch 5, sc in 2nd ch from hook and in next 3 ch, sc in next 8 sts, sl st in next st of wing top, turn—12 sts (not including the sl st).

Row 10: Ch 1, sk sl st, sc in next 12 sts, turn.

Row 11: Ch 3, sc in 2nd ch from hook and in next ch, sc in next 12 sts, sl st in next st of wing top, turn—14 sts (not including the sl st).

Row 12: Ch 1, sk sl st, sc in next 14 sts, turn.

Row 13: Ch 3, sc in 2nd ch from hook and next ch, sc in next 14 sts, sl st in next st of wing top, turn—16 sts (not including the sl st).

Row 14: Ch 1, sk sl st, sc in next 16 sts, turn.

Row 15: Ch 3, sc in 2nd ch from hook and next ch, sc in next 16 sts, sl st in next st of wing top, turn—18 sts (not including the sl st).

Row 16: Ch 1, sk sl st, sc in next 18 sts, turn.

Row 17: Ch 3, sc in 2nd ch from hook and next ch, sc in next 18 sts, sl st in next st of wing top, turn—20 sts (not including the sl st).

Row 18: Ch 1, sk sl st, sc in next 20 sts, turn.

Row 19: Ch 3, sc in 2nd ch from hook and next ch, sc in next 20 sts, sl st in next st of wing top, turn—22 sts (not including the sl st).

Row 20: Ch 1, sk sl st, sc in next 22 sts, turn.

Row 21: Ch 3, sc in 2nd ch from hook and next ch, sc in next 22 sts, sl st in next st of wing top, turn—24 sts (not including the sl st).

Row 22: Ch 1, sk sl st, sc in next 24 sts, turn.

Row 23: Ch 3, sc in 2nd ch from hook and next ch, sc in next 24 sts, sl st in next st of wing top, turn—26 sts (not including the sl st).

Row 24: Ch 1, sk sl st, sc in next 24 sts, turn; leave last 2 sts unworked—24 sts.

Row 25: Ch 1, sc in next 24 sts, sl st in next st of wing top, turn.

Row 26: Ch 1, sk sl st, sc in next 21 sts; leave last 3 sts unworked, turn—21 sts.

Row 27: Ch 1, sc in next 21 sts, sl st in next st of wing top, turn.

Row 28: Ch 1, sk sl st, sc in next 18 sts; leave last 3 sts unworked, turn—18 sts.

Row 29: Ch 1, sc in next 18 sts, sl st in next st of wing top, turn.

Row 30: Ch 1, sk sl st, sc in next 15 sts; leave last 3 sts unworked, turn—15 sts.

Row 31: Ch 1, sc in next 15 sts, sl st in next st of wing top, turn.

Row 32: Ch 1, sk sl st, sc in next 12 sts; leave last 3 sts unworked, turn—12 sts.

Row 33: Ch 1, sc in next 12 sts, sl st in next st of wing top.

Fasten off. Sew wings on back of the body in desired position.

Scan to watch a video tutorial on how to make the Raven's legs.

LEGS

Cut 2 pieces of wire about 18" (45.5 cm) long.

Bend the wire about 6" (15 cm) from one end, then bend the wire back on itself. Use pliers to squeeze the bend into a point for one claw. Repeat for three more claws, bending the claws so that one points back and the other three point forward. Wrap the working end of the wire around the center of the loops to secure them in place, and bend the wire back up to be beside the original 6" (15 cm) of wire.

Twist the two wire ends together. Bend the wire as needed to balance the raven so that it stands freely on the wire claws.

Optional: You can wrap long strands of gray yarn around the wire and the claws to add more detail; just be sure to wrap very tightly and stop wrapping before the tips of the claws to keep the sharp points.

Baby DraGoyle

Designed by Jodie Chadwick of Handmade By Jodie

Cute but fierce! This baby DraGoyle is a creature straight out of the fantastical world, ready to protect your treasures—or your heart—at a moment's notice.

Skill Level

Measurements

- Dragon made with worsted weight yarn (#4 medium): measures approx. 6" (15 cm) tall with 12" (30.5 cm) wingspan.

Yarn

- Worsted weight yarn (#4 medium) in light gray and dark gray.
- *Shown:* I Love This Yarn (7 oz/198 g, 355 yd/324 m, 100% acrylic) in Gray Mist (200) and Grey Beard (201)
- Less than 1 skein of each color is required.

Crochet Hook

- 2.75 mm (size C/2). *Note:* This is my preferred hook size, but you may need to use a different size if you are prone to loose or tight tension.

Materials

Stuffing
15 mm safety eyes
18-gauge wire, about 1 yd (1 m)

Notions

Scissors
Stitch markers
Tapestry needle
Pins

Gauge

Gauge is not critical for this project.

BACK FEET (MAKE 2)

Claw (make 3 per foot)

With light gray yarn, make a magic ring.

Rnd 1: Work 4 sc into the ring; do not join, work in continuous rnds (spiral).

Place a marker in last st made to indicate end of rnd. Move marker up as each rnd is completed.

Rnd 2: [2 sc in next st, sc in next st] 2 times—6 sts.

Change to dark gray yarn.

Rnd 3: Sc in each st around.

Fasten off first and second claw.

Do not fasten off third claw.

Join Claws

Rnd 4: Sc in next 3 sts of third claw, sc in next 3 sts of second claw, sc in all 6 sts of first claw, sc in remaining 3 sts of second claw, sc in remaining 3 sts of third claw—18 sts.

Foot

Rnds 5–7: Sc in each st around (3 rnds).

Rnd 8: [Sc2tog, sc in next 7 sts] 2 times—16 sts.

Rnd 9: [Sc2tog, sc in next 6 sts] 2 times—14 sts.

Stuff foot firmly.

Rnd 10: [Sc2tog, sc in next 5 sts] 2 times—12 sts.

Rnd 11: Sc in each st around.

Rnd 12: [Sc2tog] 6 times—6 sts.

Fasten off.

BACK LEGS (MAKE 2)

With dark gray yarn, make a magic ring.

Rnd 1: Work 6 sc into the ring; do not join, work in continuous rnds (spiral).

Place a marker in last st made to indicate end of rnd. Move marker up as each rnd is completed.

Rnd 2: 2 sc in next 6 sts—12 sts.

Rnd 3: [2 sc in next st, sc in next st] 6 times—18 sts.

Rnds 4–6: Sc in each st around (3 rnds).

Rnd 7: [Sc in next st, sc2tog] 6 times—12 sts.

Rnds 8 and 9: Sc in each st around (2 rnds).

Rnd 10: [Sc in next 4 sts, sc2tog] 2 times—10 sts.

Fasten off, leaving a long tail for sewing.

Stuff leg lightly.

Sew a back leg to each back foot, sewing so that the leg opening covers Rnds 1–3 on top of the foot.

BODY

With dark gray yarn, make a magic ring.

Rnd 1: Work 6 sc into the ring; do not join, work in continuous rnds (spiral).

Place a marker in last st made to indicate end of rnd. Move marker up as each rnd is completed.

Rnd 2: 2 sc in next 6 sts—12 sts.

Rnd 3: 2 sc in each st around—24 sts.

Rnds 4–7: Sc in each st around (4 rnds).

Rnd 8: [Sc in next 2 sts, sc2tog] 6 times—18 sts.

Rnds 9–11: Sc in each st around (3 rnds).

Rnd 12: [Sc in next st, sc2tog] 6 times—12 sts.

Rnds 13–15: Sc in each st around (3 rnds).

Fasten off.

Stuff body firmly.

FRONT LEGS (MAKE 2)

Rnds 1–4: Make and join 3 claws as for back legs—18 sts.

Foot

Rnds 5 and 6: Sc in each st around (2 rnds).

Rnd 7: [Sc in next st, sc2tog] 6 times—12 sts.

Stuff foot lightly.

Rnd 8: [Sc2tog] 3 times, [sc in next st, 2 sc in next st] 3 times.

Rnd 9: [Sc2tog] 2 times, [sc in next 2 sts, 2 sc in next st] 2 times, sc in last 2 sts.

Rnd 10: Hdc in next 3 sts, sc in last 9 sts.

Stuff leg and continue to add stuffing as work progresses.

Rnd 11: [Sc in next 4 sts, sc2tog] 2 times—10 sts.

Rnds 12–17: Sc in each st around (6 rnds).

Rnd 18: [Sc2tog] 5 times—5 sts.

Fasten off, leaving a long tail for sewing.

HEAD

With dark gray yarn, ch 5.

Rnd 1: 2 sc in 2nd ch from hook, sc in next 2 ch, 4 sc in last ch; working along opposite side of foundation ch, sc in next 2 ch, 2 sc in next ch—12 sts.

Place a marker in last st made to indicate end of rnd. Move marker up as each rnd is completed.

Rnd 2: 2 sc in each of first 2 sts, sc in next 2 sts, 2 sc in each of next 4 sts, sc in next 2 sts, 2 sc in each of last 2 sts—20 sts.

Rnds 3–6: Sc in each st around (4 rnds).

Rnd 7: Sc in first 2 sts, 2 sc in each of next 3 sts, sc in next st, 2 sc in each of next 3 sts, sc in last 11 sts—26 sts.

Rnd 8: Sc in first 2 sts, [sc in next st, 2 sc in next st] 3 times, sc in next st, [2 sc in next st, sc in next st] 3 times, sc in last 11 sts—32 sts.

Rnd 9: [Sc in next 7 sts, 2 sc in next st] 4 times—36 sts.

Rnds 10–14: Sc in each st around (5 rnds).

Rnd 15: [Sc in next 4 sts, sc2tog] 6 times—30 sts.

Insert safety eyes between Rnds 8 and 9. Stuff head firmly.

Rnd 16: [Sc in next 3 sts, sc2tog] 6 times—24 sts.

Rnd 17: [Sc in next 2 sts, sc2tog] 6 times—18 sts.

Rnd 18: [Sc in next st, sc2tog] 6 times—12 sts.

Rnd 19: [Sc2tog] 6 times—6 sts.

Fasten off.

EARS (MAKE 2)

With dark gray yarn, make a magic ring.

Rnd 1: Work 6 sc into the ring; do not join, work in continuous rnds (spiral).

Place a marker in last st made to indicate end of rnd. Move marker up as each rnd is completed.

Rnd 2: 2 sc in each of next 3 sts, ch 2, 2 sc in each of last 3 sts—12 sts and 1 ch-2 sp.

Fold piece in half; working through both thicknesses work 2 sc across edge; leave remaining sts unworked.

Fasten off, leaving a long tail for sewing.

HORNS (MAKE 2)

With light gray yarn, make a magic ring.

Rnd 1: Work 6 sc into the ring; do not join, work in continuous rnds (spiral).

Place a marker in last st made to indicate end of rnd. Move marker up as each rnd is completed.

Rnds 2 and 3: Sc in each st around (2 rnds).

Fasten off, leaving a long tail.

TAIL

With dark gray yarn, make a magic ring.

Rnd 1: Work 4 sc into the ring; do not join, work in continuous rnds (spiral).

Place a marker in last st made to indicate end of rnd. Move marker up as each rnd is completed.

Rnd 2: [2 sc in next st, sc in next st] 2 times—6 sts.

Rnd 3: Sc in each st around.

Rnd 4: 2 sc in next st, sc in next 5 sts—7 sts.

Rnds 5–9: Sc in each st around (5 rnds).

Start stuffing tail and continue adding stuffing as work progresses.

Rnd 10: 2 sc in next st, sc in next 6 sts—8 sts.

Rnds 11–14: Sc in each st around (4 rnds).

Rnd 15: [2 sc in next st, sc in next 3 sts] 2 times—10 sts.

Rnds 16–19: Sc in each st around (4 rnds).

Rnd 20: [2 sc in next st, sc in next 4 sts] 2 times—12 sts.

Rnds 21–24: Sc in each st around (4 rnds).

Rnd 25: [Sc in next 3 sts, 2 sc in next st] 3 times—15 sts.

Rnds 26 and 27: Sc in each st around (2 rnds).

Rnd 28: [Sc in next 4 sts, 2 sc in next st] 3 times—18 sts.

Rnd 29: 2 sc in each of next 3 sts, sc in next 15 sts—21 sts.

Rnd 30: [Sc in next st, 2 sc in next st] 3 times, sc in next 15 sts—24 sts.

Fasten off, leaving a long tail.

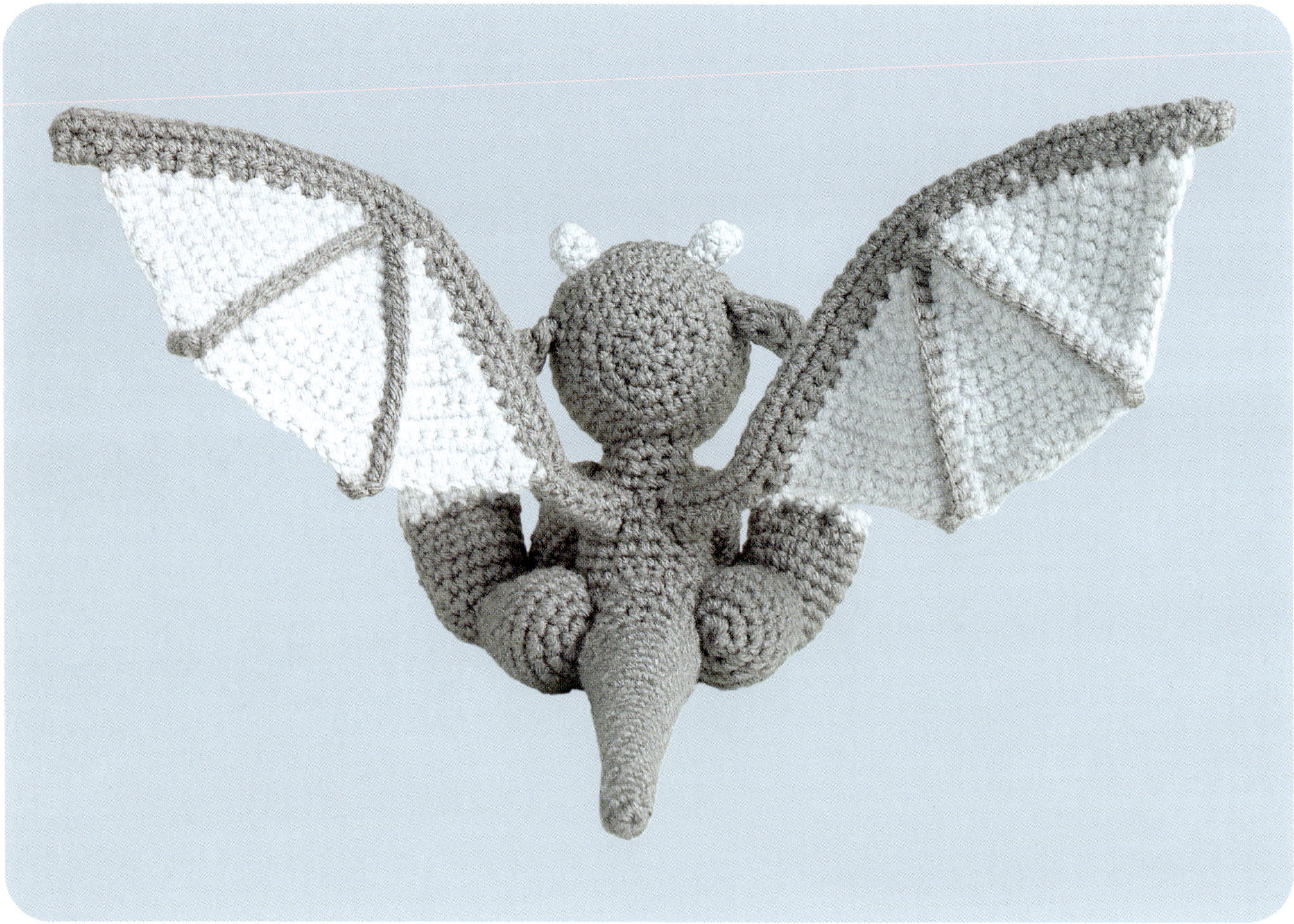

ASSEMBLY

Ears

Sew ears to Rnds 13 and 14 of the head, with the top of the ears in line with the eyes.

Back Legs

Sew back legs between Rnds 4 and 7 of the body. Only sew the first 4 or 5 rnds of the leg to the body. They should be approx. 7 to 8 sts apart at the back of the body; this will angle the feet outwards to make room for the front legs. Make sure the bottom of the body and the legs are level so the DraGoyle will sit flat.

Front Legs

Sew front legs between Rnds 12 and 15 of the body. The feet should sit flat and level with the body and back legs.

Head

I feel the head is easier to attach after the wings, but of course this is personal preference.

WINGS (MAKE 2)

Notes:

1. Each wing is made from 3 wing panels.
2. Three wing panels are joined together along their side edges to form one curved wing.
3. A wing arm is worked onto each wing to form a right wing and a left wing.

Wing Panels (make 3 per wing)

With light gray, ch 2.

Row 1: Sc in 2nd ch from hook, turn—1 st.

Row 2: Ch 1, 2 sc in st, turn—2 sts.

Row 3: Ch 1, 2 sc in each of next 2 sts, turn—4 sts.

Row 4: Ch 1, sc in each st across, turn.

Row 5: Ch 1, 2 sc in first st, sc in each st to last st, 2 sc in last st, turn—6 sts.

Rows 6 and 7: Ch 1, sc in each st across, turn (2 rows).

Rows 8–10: Rep Rows 5–7—8 sts.

Row 11: Rep Row 5—10 sts.

Row 12: Ch 2, dc in first st, hdc in next st, sc in next st, hdc in next st, dc in next 2 sts, hdc in next st, sc in next st, hdc in next st, dc in last st, do not turn—10 sts.

Row 13: Ch 1, sc evenly spaced along long side edge of wing, 4 sc in tip, work the same number of sc (as along first long side edge) along next long side edge.

Fasten off.

Join Wing Panels

Place wing panels on a flat surface, with ending tails on the left, the same side of all wing panels facing you and sts along side edges matching. Place a marker in the space between the first 2 sts and second 2 sts at the tip of each wing panel. Also place a marker on the side of the wings facing you, to indicate front of wing.

Join the side edges of the first two wing panels as follows: With dark gray and beginning at tip marker of each wing panel, working in FLO of both thicknesses, sc in each st across side edge to join panels together; ch 3, turn the joined wing panels over. Working back along same side edge, and working in the free back loops, sc in each st across.

Fasten off.

Rep to join third wing panel to second wing panel. Remove markers at tip of wings. Repeat with the remaining three panels to make the second wing.

Scan to watch a video tutorial on how to attach the wing panels.

WING ARMS

Make sure the stitch marker that indicates the front of the wing is facing you before working the first row of each wing arm. Make a right wing from one set of 3 joined wing panels and make a left wing from the other set of 3 joined wing panels.

Right Wing

Leaving a long beginning tail, with dark gray, ch 6.

Row 1: Beginning at bottom corner of the outer wing panel and working along side edge of wing panel, sc in each st across to the "dip" in the middle of the wing, work hdc, 2 dc, hdc in the "dip," sc in each st across remainder of wing, turn.

Row 2: Ch 3, sc in 2nd ch from hook and in next ch, sc in each st across, sc in each ch of beginning ch-6, turn.

Rows 3–6: Sc in each st across, turn (4 rows).

Fasten off, leaving a very long tail for sewing wing arm over wire and for sewing to the body.

Left Wing

Leaving a long beginning tail, with dark gray, ch 2.

Row 1: Beginning at bottom corner of the outer wing panel and working along side edge of wing panel, sc in each st across to the "dip" in the middle of the wing, work hdc, 2 dc, hdc in the "dip," sc in each st across remainder of wing, turn.

Row 2: Ch 7, sc in 2nd ch from hook and in next 5 ch, sc in each st across, sc in each ch of beginning ch-2.

Rows 3–6: Sc in each st across (4 rows).

Fasten off, leaving a very long tail for sewing wing arm over wire and for sewing to the body.

Note: Each end of the arm juts out longer than the actual wing panels. There is a short side and a long side. The long side is the one which will be sewn onto the body.

Fold the wing arm over so that the edge of the wing arm touches the edge of the wing panels (**Row 6 and Row 1**); this will create a tube for the wire to be inserted. Using your long tail, sew all the way along to secure. *Do not sew the ends closed.*

I used 18-gauge wire. Your wire needs to be long enough to extend over both of the wings and the body with 1" (2.5 cm) extending beyond each end. The 1" (2.5 cm) extensions will be used to create a loop at each end so that the wire does not poke through the yarn.

Once you have cut your wire, poke the wire into the back of the body between Rnds 9 and 10. Make sure there is an even amount of wire sticking out of both sides of the dragon. You can now slide the wire into the wings. You need to angle the wings upwards to be able to sew them to the body easily.

Sew the wing arm to the body around where the wire was inserted.

Once the wings are secured, you can trim the wire if needed. Leave 1" (2.5 cm) at each end. Push the wing arm down the length of the wire a little bit so you can bend the end of the wire into a loop; now cover the loop with the wing arm and sew the end closed.

You can opt to not use wire.

Fierce Dragon

Designed by Jodie Chadwick of Handmade By Jodie

No romantasy is complete without a dragon—majestic, fierce, and brimming with untold power. This crocheted creature stands ready to defend your castle, unleash fury upon your enemies, and breathe life into the most epic of tales. With every stitch, you summon a force that commands both respect and awe. But beware: while the dragon may be untamable, they might just become your fiercest ally and most loyal companion.

Skill Level

Measurements

- Dragon made with worsted weight yarn (#4 medium): measures approx. 48" (122 cm) long, 22" (56 cm) tall to top of head, with 48" (122 cm) wingspan.

Yarn

- Worsted weight yarn (#4 medium) in primary and accent colors of your choice.
- *Shown:* Print I Love This Yarn (5 oz/142 g, 252 yd/230 m, 100% acrylic) in Red Tweed (822)
- I Love This Yarn (7 oz/198 g, 355 yd/324 m, 100% acrylic) in Black (30)
- 7 skeins of worsted weight yarn in primary color and 3 skeins of worsted weight yarn in accent color are required.

Crochet Hook

- 2.75 mm (size C/2). *Note:* This is my preferred hook size, but you may need to use a different size if you are prone to loose or tight tension.

Materials

Stuffing
30 mm slit pupil safety eyes
14-gauge wire, about 1 yd (1 m)

Notions

Scissors
Stitch markers
Tapestry needle
Pins

Gauge

Gauge is not critical for this project.

FEET (MAKE 4)

Claws (make 3 per foot)

With accent color, make a magic ring.

Rnd 1: Work 4 sc into the ring; do not join, work in continuous rnds (spiral).

Place a marker in last st made to indicate end of rnd. Move marker up as each rnd is completed.

Rnd 2: [2 sc in next st, sc in next st] 2 times—6 sts.

Rnds 3 and 4: Sc in each st around (2 rnds).

Change to primary color (for toe).

Rnd 5: 2 sc in each st around—12 sts.

Rnd 6: Sc in each st around.

Rnd 7: [Sc in next st, 2 sc in next st] 6 times—18 sts.

Rnd 8: Sc in next 3 sts, [sc2tog] 6 times, sc in last 3 sts—12 sts.

Rnd 9: Sc in each st around.

Rnd 10: 2 sc in next st, sc in next 3 sts, [sc2tog] 2 times, sc in next 3 sts, 2 sc in next st—12 sts.

Rnds 11 and 12: Sc in each st around (2 rnds).

Knuckles

Rnd 13: [Sc2tog] 2 times, sc in next st, 2 hdc in each of next 4 sts, sc in next st, sc2tog—13 sts.

Rnd 14: Sc in each st around.

Rnd 15: 2 sc in each of next 3 sts, [hdc2tog] 2 times, sc in next st, [hdc2tog] 2 times, 2 sc in next st—13 sts.

Rnd 16: 2 sc in each of next 4 sts, sc in next 2 sts, sc2tog, sc in next st, sc2tog, sc in next 2 sts—15 sts.

Rnd 17: Sc in each st around.

Fasten off first and second claw.

Do not fasten off third claw.

Stuff claws and toes firmly, shaping the knuckles.

Join Toes/Claws

Make sure all knuckles are facing upwards as you join each toe/claw.

Rnd 18: With third toe still on hook, hold second toe next to third toe (make sure the knuckles of both toes are facing upwards), sc in closest st of second toe and in next 6 sts; hold first toe next to the second toe (make sure that the knuckles of all toes are facing upwards), sc in closest st of first toe and in next 14 sts; sc in next 8 sts of second (middle) toe, sc in next 8 sts of third toe.

Move beg of rnd marker to last sc made to indicate new end of rnd.

Stuff the foot firmly as you work your way up.

Rnds 19–22: Sc in each st around (4 rnds)—45 sts.

Rnd 23: Sc in next 21 sts, sc3tog, sc in next 18 sts, sc3tog—41 sts.

Rnd 24: Sc in next 5 sts, sc3tog, sc in next 6 sts, sc3tog, sc in next 4 sts, sc2tog, sc in next 16 sts, sc2tog—35 sts.

Rnd 25: Sc3tog, sc in next 12 sts, sc3tog, sc in next 17 sts—31 sts.

Rnd 26: Sc2tog, sc in next 10 sts, [sc2tog] 3 times, sc in next 9 sts, [sc2tog] 2 times—25 sts.

Rnds 27–32: Sc in each st around (6 rnds).

Rnd 33: [Sc in next 3 sts, sc2tog] 5 times—20 sts.

Rnd 34: Sc in each st around.

Rnd 35: [Sc in next 2 sts, sc2tog] 5 times—15 sts.

Rnd 36: [Sc in next st, sc2tog] 5 times—10 sts.

Fasten off, leaving a long tail. Thread tail through sts of last rnd and pull tight to close opening. Weave in tail securely.

BACK LEGS (MAKE 2)

With primary color, make a magic ring.

Rnd 1: Work 6 sc into the ring; do not join, work in continuous rnds (spiral).

Place a marker in last st made to indicate end of rnd. Move marker up as each rnd is completed.

Rnd 2: 2 sc in next 6 sts—12 sts.

Rnd 3: [2 sc in next st, sc in next st] 6 times—18 sts.

Rnd 4: [Sc in next 2 sts, 2 sc in next st] 6 times—24 sts.

Rnd 5: [Sc in next 3 sts, 2 sc in next st] 6 times—30 sts.

Rnd 6: [Sc in next 4 sts, 2 sc in next st] 6 times—36 sts.

Rnd 7: [Sc in next 5 sts, 2 sc in next st] 6 times—42 sts.

Rnd 8: [Sc in next 6 sts, 2 sc in next st] 6 times—48 sts.

Rnd 9: [Sc in next 7 sts, 2 sc in next st] 6 times—54 sts.

Rnds 10–18: Sc in each st around (9 rnds).

Rnd 19: [Sc in next 7 sts, sc2tog] 6 times—48 sts.

Rnds 20–25: Sc in each st around (6 rnds).

Rnd 26: [Sc in next 6 sts, sc2tog] 6 times—42 sts.

Rnds 27–32: Sc in each st around (6 rnds).

Rnd 33: [Sc in next 5 sts, sc2tog] 6 times—36 sts.

Rnds 34–37: Sc in each st around (4 rnds).

Knee Joint

Knee joint is worked in short rows. Do not ch-1 at the end of each row before turning.

Row 38: Turn, sc in next 18 sts; leave remaining sts unworked—18 sts.

Row 39: Turn, sc in each st across to last st; leave last st unworked—17 sts.

Rows 40–42: Rep Row 39 for 3 more times—14 sts in Row 42.

Rnd 43: Turn, sc in each st around including the unworked sts from previous rows—36 sts.

Stuff the leg firmly and continue stuffing as work progresses.

Rnd 44: [Sc in next 4 sts, sc2tog] 6 times—30 sts.

Rnds 45–56: Sc in each st around (12 rnds).

Ankle Joint

We will now create the bend for the ankle joint. The short rows need to be on the opposite side of the leg from the knee joint. You may need to add or remove a st or two to get to the right position. Do not ch-1 before turning.

Row 57: Turn, sc in next 15 sts; leave remaining sts unworked—15 sts.

Row 58: Turn, sc in each st across to last st; leave last st unworked—14 sts.

Row 59: Rep Row 58—13 sts.

Rnd 60: Turn, sc in each st around including the unworked sts from previous rows—30 sts.

Rnds 61 and 62: Sc in each st around (2 rnds).

Rnd 63: [Sc in next 3 sts, sc2tog] 6 times—24 sts.

Rnds 64–76: Sc in each st around (13 rnds).

Fasten off, leaving a long tail for sewing to foot.

FRONT LEGS (MAKE 2)

Work same as Back Leg through Rnd 33—36 sts in Rnd 33.

Rnds 34–38: Sc in each st around (5 rnds).

Elbow Joint

Elbow joint is worked in short rows. Do not ch-1 at the end of each row before turning.

Row 39: Turn, sc in next 18 sts; leave remaining sts unworked—18 sts.

Row 40: Turn, sc in each st across to last st; leave last st unworked—17 sts.

Rows 41–43: Rep Row 40 for 3 more times—14 sts in Row 43.

Rnd 44: Turn, sc in each st including the unworked sts from previous rows—36 sts.

Rnds 45 and 46: Sc in each st around (2 rnds).

Stuff leg firmly and continue stuffing as work progresses.

Rnd 47: [Sc in next 4 sts, sc2tog] 6 times—30 sts.

Rnds 48–60: Sc in each st around (13 rnds).

Rnd 61: [Sc in next 8 sts, sc2tog] 3 times—27 sts.

Rnds 62–66: Sc in each st around (5 rnds).

Rnd 67: [Sc in next 7 sts, sc2tog] 3 times—24 sts.

Rnds 68–72: Sc in each st around (5 rnds).

Fasten off, leaving a long tail for sewing to foot.

TAIL AND BODY

Wire can be used throughout the body, but this is completely optional.

With primary color, make a magic ring.

Rnd 1: Work 5 sc into the ring; do not join, work in continuous rnds (spiral).

Place a marker in last st made to indicate end of rnd. Move marker up as each rnd is completed.

Rnd 2: Sc in each st around.

Rnd 3: 2 sc in next st, sc in each st around—6 sts.

Rnds 4 and 5: Sc in each st around (2 rnds).

Rnds 6 and 7: 2 sc in next st, sc in each st around—8 st in Rnd 7.

Rnds 8–11: Sc in each st around (4 rnds).

Rnd 12: [2 sc in next st, sc in next 3 sts] 2 times—10 sts.

Begin stuffing firmly and continue stuffing as work progresses.

Rnds 13–16: Sc in each st around (4 rnds).

Rnd 17: [2 sc in next st, sc in next 4 sts] 2 times—12 sts.

Rnds 18–21: Sc in each st around (4 rnds).

Rnd 22: [2 sc in next st, sc in next 5 sts] 2 times—14 sts.

Rnds 23–28: Sc in each st around (6 rnds).

Rnd 29: [2 sc in next st, sc in next 6 sts] 2 times—16 sts.

Rnds 30–35: Sc in each st around (6 rnds).

Rnd 36: [2 sc in next st, sc in next 7 sts] 2 times—18 sts.

Rnds 37–41: Sc in each st around (5 rnds).

Rnd 42: [Sc in next 5 sts, 2 sc in next st] 3 times—21 sts.

Rnds 43–48: Sc in each st around (6 rnds).

Rnd 49: [Sc in next 6 sts, 2 sc in next st] 3 times—24 sts.

Rnds 50–54: Sc in each st around (5 rnds).

Rnd 55: [Sc in next 7 sts, 2 sc in next st] 3 times—27 sts.

Rnds 56–60: Sc in each st around (5 rnds).

Rnd 61: [Sc in next 8 sts, 2 sc in next st] 3 times—30 sts.

Rnds 62–66: Sc in each st around (5 rnds).

Rnd 67: [Sc in next 9 sts, 2 sc in next st] 3 times—33 sts.

Rnds 68–72: Sc in each st around (5 rnds).

Rnd 73: [Sc in next 10 sts, 2 sc in next st] 3 times—36 sts.

Rnds 74–78: Sc in each st around (5 rnds).

Rnd 79: [Sc in next 11 sts, 2 sc in next st] 3 times—39 sts.

Rnds 80–84: Sc in each st around (5 rnds).

Rnd 85: [Sc in next 12 sts, 2 sc in next st] 3 times—42 sts.

Rnds 86–90: Sc in each st around (5 rnds).

Rnd 91: [Sc in next 13 sts, 2 sc in next st] 3 times—45 sts.

Rnds 92–96: Sc in each st around (5 rnds).

Rnd 97: [Sc in next 14 sts, 2 sc in next st] 3 times—48 sts.

Rnds 98–102: Sc in each st around (5 rnds).

Rnd 103: [Sc in next 7 sts, 2 sc in next st] 6 times—54 sts.

Rnds 104 and 105: Sc in each st around (2 rnds).

Form Curve

Curves are worked in short rows. Do not ch-1 at the end of each row before turning.

Row 106: DO NOT turn, sc in next 27 sts; leave remaining sts unworked—27 sts.

Row 107: Turn, sc in next 26 sts, leave last st unworked—26 sts.

Row 108: Turn, sc in each st to last st; leave last st unworked—25 sts.

Rows 109–111: Rep Rnd 108 for 3 more times—22 sts in Row 111.

Rnd 112: Sc in in each st around including the unworked sts from previous rows—54 sts.

Rnds 113–116: Sc in each st around (4 rnds).

Rnd 117: Sc in next 24 sts, [sc in next 4 sts, 2 sc in next st] 6 times—60 sts.

Rnds 118–148: Sc in each st around (31 rnds).

Rnd 149: Sc in next 24 sts, [sc in next 4 sts, sc2tog] 6 times—54 sts.

Rnds 150–153: Sc in each st around (4 rnds).

Form Curve

Curves are worked in short rows. Do not ch-1 at the end of each row before turning.

Before working Row 154, if needed, work additional sc sts to reach the side of the body opposite short Rows 106–111.

Row 154: Turn, sc in next 27 sts; leave remaining sts unworked—27 sts.

Row 155: Turn, sc in each st to last st; leave last st unworked—26 sts.

Rows 156–170: Rep Row 155 for 15 more times—11 sts in Row 170.

Rnd 171: Sc in in each st around including the unworked sts from previous rows—54 sts.

Rnds 172–178: Sc in each st around (7 rnds).

Rnd 179: [Sc in next 7 sts, sc2tog] 6 times—48 sts.

Rnds 180–186: Sc in each st around (7 rnds).

Form Curve

Curves are worked in short rows. Do not ch-1 at the end of each row before turning.

Before working Row 186, if needed, unravel st and move the end of rnd marker back a couple of sts to be in line with short Rows 154–170.

Row 187: DO NOT turn, sc in next 21 sts; leave remaining sts unworked—21 sts.

Row 188: Turn, sc in next 24 sts; leave remaining sts unworked—24 sts.

Row 189: Turn, sc in each st to last st; leave last st unworked—23 sts.

Rows 190–192: Rep Row 189 for 3 more times—20 sts in Row 192.

Rnd 193: Sc in each st around including the unworked sts from previous rows—48 sts.

Rnds 194 and 195: Sc in each st around (2 rnds).

Rnd 196: [Sc in next 6 sts, sc2tog] 6 times—42 sts.

Rnds 197–201: Sc in each st around (5 rnds).

Rnd 202: [Sc in next 5 sts, sc2tog] 6 times—36 sts.

Rnds 203–213: Sc in each st around (11 rnds).

Fasten off, leaving a long tail for sewing to the head.

HEAD

With primary color, ch 5.

Rnd 1: 2 sc in 2nd ch from hook, sc in next 2 ch, 4 sc in last ch; working along opposite side of foundation ch, sc in next 2 ch, 2 sc in next ch—12 sts.

Place a marker in last st made to indicate end of rnd. Move marker up as each rnd is completed.

Rnd 2: Sc in next st, 2 sc in next st, sc in next 2 sts, 2 sc in next st, sc in next 2 sts, 2 sc in next st, sc in next 2 sts, 2 sc in next st, sc in next st—16 sts.

Rnd 3: [Sc in next st, 2 sc in each of next 2 sts, sc in next 3 sts, 2 sc in each of next 2 sts] 2 times—24 sts.

Rnd 4: Sc in next 2 sts, 2 sc in each of next 2 sts, sc in next 5 sts, 2 sc in each of next 2 sts, sc in next 3 sts, 2 sc in each of next 2 sts, sc in next 5 sts, 2 sc in each of next 2 sts, sc in next st—32 sts.

Rnds 5–9: Sc in each st around (5 rnds).

Rnd 10: [Sc in next 7 sts, 2 sc in next st] 4 times—36 sts.

Rnds 11 and 12: Sc in each st around (2 rnds).

Rnd 13: Sc in next 3 sts, 2 sc in next st, [sc in next 8 sts, 2 sc in next st] 3 times, sc in next 5 sts—40 sts.

Rnds 14 and 15: Sc in each st around (2 rnds).

Rnd 16: Sc in next 6 sts, 2 sc in next st, [sc in next 9 sts, 2 sc in next st] 3 times, sc in next 3 sts—44 sts.

Rnd 17: Sc in each st around.

Rnd 18: Sc in next 7 sts, 2 sc in next st, [sc in next 10 sts, 2 sc in next st] 3 times, sc in next 3 sts—48 sts.

Rnd 19: Sc in each st around.

Rnd 20: Sc in next 5 sts, 2 sc in next st, [sc in next 11 sts, 2 sc in next st] 3 times, sc in next 6 sts—52 sts.

Rnd 21: Sc in each st around.

Rnd 22: Sc in next 6 sts, 2 sc in next st, [sc in next 12 sts, 2 sc in next st] 3 times, sc in next 6 sts—56 sts.

Rnd 23: Sc in each st around.

Rnd 24: [Sc in next 13 sts, 2 sc in next st] 4 times—60 sts.

Rnd 25: Sc in each st around.

Rnd 26: [Sc in next 14 sts, 2 sc in next st] 4 times—64 sts.

Rnd 27: Sc in each st around.

Rnd 28: [Sc in next 15 sts, 2 sc in next st] 4 times—68 sts.

Rnds 29–37: Sc in each st around (9 rnds).

Rnd 38: Sc in next 12 sts, sc2tog, sc in next 22 sts, sc2tog, sc in next 30 sts—66 sts.

Rnd 39: [Sc in next 9 sts, sc2tog] 6 times—60 sts.

Rnd 40: [Sc in next 8 sts, sc2tog] 6 times—54 sts.

Rnd 41: [Sc in next 7 sts, sc2tog] 6 times—48 sts.

Insert safety eyes between Rnds 26 and 27 approx. 19–21 sts apart.

Stuff head firmly.

Rnd 42: [Sc in next 6 sts, sc2tog] 6 times—42 sts.

Rnd 43: [Sc in next 5 sts, sc2tog] 6 times—36 sts.

Rnd 44: [Sc in next 4 sts, sc2tog] 6 times—30 sts.

Rnd 45: [Sc in next 3 sts, sc2tog] 6 times—24 sts.

Rnd 46: [Sc in next 2 sts, sc2tog] 6 times—18 sts.

Rnd 47: [Sc in next st, sc2tog] 6 times—12 sts.

Rnd 48: [Sc2tog] 6 times—6 sts.

Fasten off, leaving a long tail. Thread tail through sts of last rnd and pull tight to close opening. Weave in tail securely.

NOSTRILS (MAKE 2)

With primary color, ch 6.

Row 1: Sc in 2nd ch from hook, hdc in next 3 ch, sc in last ch—5 sts.

Fasten off, leaving a long tail for sewing to the muzzle.

EYELIDS (MAKE 2)

With primary color, ch 10.

Row 1: Sc in 2nd ch from hook, sc in next ch, hdc in next 2 ch, dc in next ch, hdc in next 2 ch, sc in last 2 ch—9 sts.

Fasten off, leaving a long tail for sewing to the head.

LARGE HORNS (MAKE 2)

With accent color, make a magic ring.

Rnd 1: Work 4 sc into the ring; do not join, work in continuous rnds (spiral).

Place a marker in last st made to indicate end of rnd. Move marker up as each rnd is completed.

Rnd 2: 2 sc in next st, sc in each st around—5 sts.

Rnds 3 and 4: Rep Rnd 2 twice—7 sts in Rnd 4.

Rnd 5: Sc in each st around.

Rnd 6: 2 sc in next st, sc in next 6 sts– 8 sts.

Rnd 7: Sc in each st around.

Rnd 8: 2 sc in each of next 2 sts, sc in next 6 sts—10 sts.

Rnds 9 and 10: Sc in each st around (2 rnds).

Rnd 11: 2 sc in each of next 2 sts, sc in each st around—12 sts.

Rnds 12–14: Rep Rnds 9–11—14 sts in Rnd 14.

Rnds 15–17: Sc in each st around (3 rnds).

Rnd 18: Rep Rnd 11—16 sts.

Rnds 19–21: Sc in each st around (3 rnds).

Fasten off, leaving a long tail for sewing to the head.

Stuff firmly.

SIDE HORNS (MAKE 4)

With accent color, make a magic ring.

Rnd 1: Work 5 sc into the ring; do not join, work in continuous rnds (spiral).

Place a marker in last st made to indicate end of rnd. Move marker up as each rnd is completed.

Rnd 2: 2 sc in next st, sc in each st around—6 sts.

Rnd 3: Sc in each st around.

Rnds 4 and 5: Rep Rnd 2 twice—8 sts in Rnd 5.

Rnd 6: Sc in each st around.

Rnd 7: [2 sc in next st, sc in next 3 sts] 2 times—10 sts.

Rnd 8: Sc in each st around.

Rnd 9: [2 sc in next st, sc in next 4 sts] 2 times—12 sts.

Rnds 10–13: Sc in each st around (4 rnds).

Fasten off, leaving a long tail for sewing to the head. Stuff lightly.

FRONT HORNS (MAKE 2)

With primary color, make a magic ring.

Rnd 1: Work 5 sc into the ring; do not join, work in continuous rnds (spiral).

Place a marker in last st made to indicate end of rnd. Move marker up as each rnd is completed.

Rnd 2: 2 sc in next st, sc in each st around—6 sts.

Rnds 3 and 4: Rep Rnd 2 twice—8 sts in Rnd 4.

Rnd 5: [2 sc in next st, sc in next 3 sts] 2 times—10 sts.

Rnds 6–8: Sc in each st around (3 rnds).

Fasten off, leaving a long tail for sewing to the head. Stuff lightly.

SMALL MUZZLE SPIKES (MAKE 2)

With primary color, make a magic ring.

Rnd 1: Work 4 sc into the ring; do not join, work in continuous rnds (spiral).

Place a marker in last st made to indicate end of rnd. Move marker up as each rnd is completed.

Rnd 2: 2 sc in next st, sc in each st around—5 sts.

Rnd 3: Sc in each st around.

Fasten off, leaving a long tail for sewing to the muzzle.

LARGE MUZZLE SPIKE

With primary color, make a magic ring.

Rnd 1: Work 4 sc into the ring; do not join, work in continuous rnds (spiral).

Place a marker in last st made to indicate end of rnd. Move marker up as each rnd is completed.

Rnd 2: 2 sc in next st, sc in each st around—5 sts.

Rnds 3–5: Rep Rnd 2 for 3 more times—8 sts in Rnd 5.

Fasten off, leaving a long tail for sewing to the muzzle.

CHEST PATCH

With accent color, ch 13.

Row 1: Sc in 2nd ch from hook and in each ch across, turn—12 sts.

Rows 2–12: Ch 1, working in BLO, hdc in each st across, turn (11 rows).

Row 13: Ch 1, working in BLO, (hdc, 2 sc) in first st, hdc in next 10 sts, (hdc, 2 sc) in last st, turn—14 sts.

Rows 14–47: Ch 1, working in BLO, hdc in each st across, turn (34 rows).

Rnd 48: Ch 1, working in BLO, hdc2tog, hdc in next 10 sts, hdc2tog, turn—12 sts.

Rnd 49: Ch 1, working in BLO, hdc2tog, hdc in next 8 sts, hdc2tog, turn—10 sts.

Rnds 50–53: Ch 1, working in BLO, hdc in each st across, turn (4 rows).

Rnd 54: Ch 1, working in BLO, hdc2tog, hdc in next 6 sts, hdc2tog, turn—8 sts.

Rnd 55: Ch 1, working in BLO, hdc in each st across, turn.

Fasten off, leaving a very long tail for sewing to the body.

WINGS (MAKE 2)

Notes:

1. Each wing is made from 4 wing panels.
2. Four wing panels are joined together along side edges to form one curved wing.
3. A wing arm is worked onto each wing to form a right wing and a left wing.

Wing Panels (make 4 per wing)

With primary color, ch 2.

Row 1: Sc in 2nd ch from hook, turn—1 st.

Row 2: Ch 1, 2 sc in st, turn—2 sts.

Row 3: Ch 1, 2 sc in each of next 2 sts, turn—4 sts.

Row 4: Ch 1, sc in each st across, turn.

Row 5: Ch 1, 2 sc in first st, sc in each st to last st, 2 sc in last st, turn—6 sts.

Rows 6 and 7: Ch 1, sc in each st across, turn (2 rows).

Rows 8–10: Rep Rows 5–7—8 sts.

Row 11: Rep Row 5—10 sts.

Rows 12–14: Ch 1, sc in each st across, turn (3 rows).

Row 15: Ch 1, 2 sc in next st, sc in next 8 sts, 2 sc in next st, turn—12 sts.

Rows 16 and 17: Ch 1, sc in each st across, turn (2 rows).

Row 18: 2 sc in next st, sc in each st to last st, 2 sc in last st—14 sts.

Rows 19–30: Rep Rows 16–18 for 4 more times—22 sts in Row 30.

Rows 31–35: Ch 1, sc in each st across, turn (5 rows).

Row 36: 2 sc in next st, sc in each st to last st, 2 sc in next st—24 sts.

Rows 37–54: Rep Rows 31–36 for 3 more times—30 sts in Row 54.

Rows 55–59: Ch 1, sc in each st across, turn (5 rows).

Row 60: Ch 2, turn, tr in first 2 sts, dc in next 2 sts, hdc in next 2 sts, sc in next 2 sts, sl st in next 14 sts, sc in next 2 sts, hdc in next 2 sts, dc in next 2 sts, tr in last 2 sts, turn.

Row 61: Ch 1, sc evenly spaced along long side edge of wing, 4 sc in tip, work the same number of sc (as along first long side edge) along next long side edge.

Notes: You should have approximately 60 sc sts along each side. Make sure all wing panels have the same number of sc sts on the sides; this is what you will use to join them.

Fasten off.

Join Wing Panels

Place wing panels on a flat surface, with ending tails on the left, the same side of all wing panels facing you, and sts along side edges matching. Place a marker in the space between the first 2 sts and second 2 sts at the tip of each wing panel. Also place a marker on the side of the wings facing you, to indicate front of wing.

Join the side edges of the first two wing panels as follows:

With primary color and beginning at tip marker of each wing panel, working in FLO of both thicknesses, sc in each st across side edge to join panels together; ch 3, turn the joined wing panels over. Working back along same side edge, and working in the free back loops, sc in each st across.

Fasten off.

Rep to join third and fourth wing panel to second wing panel. Remove markers at tip of wings.

Scan to watch a video tutorial on how to attach the wing panels.

WING ARMS

Make sure the stitch marker that indicates the front of the wing is facing you before working the first row of each wing arm. Make a right wing from one set of 4 joined wing panels and make a left wing from the other set of 4 joined wing panels.

Left Wing

Leaving a long beginning tail, with primary color, ch 6.

Row 1: Beginning at bottom corner of the outer wing panel and working alongside edge of wing panel, sc in each st across, turn.

Row 2: Ch 9, sc in 2nd ch from hook and in next 7 ch, sc in each st across, sc in each ch of beginning ch-6, turn.

Rows 3–10: Sc in each st across, turn (8 rows).

Fasten off, leaving a very long tail for sewing wing arm over wire and for sewing to the body.

Right Wing

Leaving a long beginning tail, with primary color, ch 8.

Row 1: Beginning at bottom corner of the outer wing panel and working along side edge of wing panel, sc in each st across, turn.

Row 2: Ch 7, sc in 2nd ch from hook and in next 5 ch, sc in each st across, sc in each ch of beginning ch-8, turn.

Rows 3–10: Sc in each st across, turn (8 rows).

Fasten off, leaving a very long tail for sewing wing arm over wire and for sewing to the body.

Attach Wire to Arms

Each end of the arm juts out longer than the actual wing panels. There is a short side and a long side. The long side is the one which will be sewn onto the body.

Fold 14-gauge wire in half to make a double layer of wire.

Place the doubled wire along the arm and measure how much you need.

Allow an extra 1–1½" (3–4 cm) at the long end; this will be the end you poke into the body before sewing the wing onto the body.

Once you have cut your wire, lay it against the wing arm and bend it into the same shape as the wing. Make sure the fold is in the shortest side of the arm.

Now fold the flat arm part over the wire. Use the tail to sew the arm in place around the wire. I just go from front to back, back to front all the way along until the wire is completely secure. Make sure your stitch marker is facing upwards!

ASSEMBLY

Feet

Make sure your legs and feet are stuffed firmly. Sew one foot to each front leg and one to each back leg. Sew the feet to the legs so that the back of the ankle is flush with the back of the foot and the knuckles are pointing upwards.

Legs

This can be tricky, so make sure you have some good, strong pins!

- Pin all four legs to the body so all four feet sit on the floor properly.
- Pin the front legs against the curve on the chest of the dragon. They should be approx. 1" (2.5 cm) lower than the top of the body.
- Pin the back legs against the curve where the body meets the tail. Pin the right back leg so the foot is flat on the floor. Pin the left back leg angled slightly back so only the toes touch the floor. The left back leg can be straight (the same as the rest) if preferred.
- Once you are happy with the position, sew the legs to the body. Press the shoulders and hips tightly to the body and sew all around them, securing every part which touches the body.

Horns

- Sew a large horn to each side of head, between Rnds 49 and 55 and approx. 10 sts apart.
- Sew a side horn one st below and one rnd back from each large horn.
- Sew another side horn one st below and one rnd back from the previous side horns.
- Sew front horns in front of the large horns, slightly towards the middle of the head (half of the front horn should overlap in front of the large horn).

Eyelids

Sew eyelids in preferred position over top edge of eyes, depending on the look/personality you want your dragon to have.

Nostrils

Sew the nostrils to head, between Rnds 6 and 7. Curve them so they only cover approx. 3 to 4 sts.

Face Lines

With primary color, work surface sc lines between the front horns and nostrils, as follows: Attach yarn in front of front horns, * sc in next st, ch 2; rep from * to nostrils. Fasten off. Weave in the ends.

Muzzle Spikes

Sew largest muzzle spike to front of muzzle between Rnds 8 and 10. Sew the next spike one rnd away from the large spike. Sew the next spike on one rnd away.

Wings

Bend the wire for the wings at a 90-degree angle and poke it into the body directly behind the front legs approx. three-quarters of the way from the top of the body. Sew the wing arm to the body from where the wire pokes into the body up to the top of the body. Make sure you wrap a few stitches around the wire to hold the wings firmly. Also sew the wing arm to the back of the front leg for extra stability.

Chest Patch

Sew the chest patch to the dragon's chest, beginning directly under the head. The chest patch is quite stretchy, but do not stretch it too much, as you do not want to see holes.

CROCHET RESOURCES

SKILL LEVELS

 **Basic**
 **Easy**
 **Intermediate**
♥♥♥♥ **Complex**

ABBREVIATIONS

approx. = approximately
BLO = back loop(s) only
ch = chain
dc = double crochet
dc2tog (aka dc-dec) = double crochet 2 stitches together
FLO = front loop(s) only
hdc = half double crochet
hdc2tog (aka hdc-dec) = half double crochet 2 stitches together
htr = half treble crochet
rem = remain(ing)
rep = repeat
rnd(s) = round(s)
RS = right side
sc = single crochet
sc2tog (aka dec) = single crochet 2 stitches together
sc3tog = single crochet 3 stitches together
sk = skip
sl st = slip stitch
sp(s) = space(s)
st(s) = stitch(es)
tr (aka tc) = treble (triple) crochet
WS = wrong side

HOW TO READ A PATTERN

Crochet instructions are written in a shortened form, using standard abbreviations. This greatly reduces the space and overwhelming confusion that would result if the instructions were written out completely, word for word. Diagrams with symbols that represent the stitches are often given along with the written instructions, or sometimes the diagrams stand alone.

Crochet patterns are often groups of stitches that are repeated a certain number of times in a row or round. Rather than repeat the instructions for the stitch group over and over, the group is enclosed between brackets [ ] immediately followed by the number of times to work the stitches.

For example: [ch 1, sk 1, 1 dc in next st] 4 times.

This is a much shorter way to say "chain 1, skip 1 stitch, work 1 double crochet in the next stitch, chain 1, skip 1 stitch, work 1 double crochet in the next stitch, chain 1, skip 1 stitch, work 1 double crochet in the next stitch, chain 1, skip 1 stitch, work 1 double crochet in the next stitch."

Another way to indicate repeated stitch patterns is with **asterisks (*)**. This same instruction could be written: * ch 1, sk 1, 1 dc in next st, repeat from * 3 times more.

Parentheses are used to clarify or reinforce information: Ch 3 (counts as 1 dc). They may be used at the end of a row to tell you how many total stitches you should have in that row, such as (25 sc). Sometimes this information is set off with an em dash at the row end—25 sc. Parentheses are also used to tell you which side of the work you should be on: (WS) or (RS).

ESSENTIAL CROCHET TECHNIQUES

Below are instructions for the crochet techniques used in this book. Beginners can use this section to learn the skills they will need to tackle a crochet project. Refer to them whenever you need to brush up on stitches and maneuvers you've already learned. The instructions are written out completely, making them easier to understand.

Slip Knot and Chain

All crochet begins with a chain, into which is worked the foundation row for your piece. To make a chain, start with a slip knot. To make a slip knot, make a loop several inches from the end of the yarn, insert the hook through the loop, and catch the tail with the end. Draw the yarn through the loop on the hook. After the slip knot, start your chain. Wrap the yarn over the hook (yarn over) and catch it with the hook. Draw the yarn through the loop on the hook. You have now made 1 chain. Repeat the process to make a row of chains. When counting chains, do not count the slip knot at the beginning or the loop that is on the hook.

Slip Knot and Chain

Slip Stitch

The slip stitch is a very short stitch, which is mainly used to join 2 pieces of crochet together when working in rounds. To make a slip stitch, insert the hook into the specified stitch, wrap the yarn over the hook, and then draw the yarn through the stitch and the loop already on the hook.

Slip Stitch

Single Crochet

Insert the hook into the specified stitch, wrap the yarn over the hook, and draw the yarn through the stitch so there are 2 loops on the hook. Wrap the yarn over the hook again and draw the yarn through both loops. When working in single crochet, always insert the hook through both top loops of the next stitch, unless the directions specify front loop or back loop only.

Single Crochet

Half Double Crochet
Wrap the yarn over the hook, insert the hook into the specified stitch, and wrap the yarn over the hook again. Draw the yarn through the stitch so there are 3 loops on the hook. Wrap the yarn over the hook and draw it through all 3 loops at once.

Double Crochet
Wrap the yarn over the hook, insert the hook into the specified stitch, and wrap the yarn over the hook again. Draw the yarn through the stitch so there are 3 loops on the hook. Wrap the yarn over the hook again and draw it through 2 of the loops so there are now 2 loops on the hook. Wrap the yarn over the hook again and draw it through the last 2 loops.

Triple Crochet
Wrap the yarn over the hook twice, insert the hook into the specified stitch, and wrap the yarn over the hook again. Draw the yarn through the stitch so there are 4 loops on the hook. Wrap the yarn over the hook again and draw it through 2 of the loops so there are now 3 loops on the hook. Wrap the yarn over the hook again and draw it through 2 of the loops so there are now 2 loops on the hook. Wrap the yarn over the hook again and draw it through the last 2 loops.

Double Triple Crochet
Wrap the yarn over the hook 3 times, insert the hook into the specified stitch, and wrap the yarn over the hook again. Draw the yarn through the stitch so there are 5 loops on the hook. Wrap the yarn over the hook again and draw it through 2 of the loops so there are now 4 loops on the hook. Wrap the yarn over the hook again and draw it through 2 of the loops so there are now 3 loops on the hook. Wrap the yarn over the hook again and draw it through 2 of the loops so there are now 2 loops on the hook. Wrap the yarn over the hook again and draw it through the last 2 loops.

Working Through the Back Loop
This creates a distinct ridge on the side facing you. Insert the hook through the back loop only of each stitch, rather than under both loops of the stitch. Complete the stitch as usual.

Half Double Crochet

Double Crochet

Triple Crochet

Increasing and Decreasing
To shape your work, you will often increase or decrease stitches as directed by the pattern. To increase in a row or round, you crochet twice into the same stitch, thereby increasing the stitch count by 1. To increase at the end of a row, you chain extra stitches, then turn and work into those stitches, thereby increasing the stitch count.

To decrease in a row or round, you crochet 2 (or more) stitches together as directed, thereby decreasing the stitch count. The technique varies depending on which crochet stitch you are using.

Single Crochet Two Stitches Together

Single Crochet Two Stitches Together
This decreases the number of stitches in a row or round by 1. Insert the hook into the specified stitch, wrap the yarn over the hook, and draw the yarn through the stitch so there are 2 loops on the hook. Insert the hook through the next stitch, wrap the yarn over the hook, and draw the yarn through the stitch so there are 3 loops on the hook. Wrap the yarn over the hook again and draw the yarn through all the loops at once.

Double Crochet Two Stitches Together

Double Crochet Two Stitches Together
This decreases the number of stitches in a row or round by 1. Wrap the yarn over the hook, insert the hook into the specified stitch, and wrap the yarn over the hook again. Draw the yarn through the stitch so there are 3 loops on the hook. Wrap the yarn over the hook again and draw it through 2 of the loops so there are now 2 loops on the hook. Wrap the yarn over the hook and pick up a loop in the next stitch, so there are now 4 loops on the hook. Wrap the yarn over the hook and draw through 2 loops. Wrap yarn over and draw through 3 loops to complete the stitch.

Scan to watch a video tutorial on how to make an invisible decrease when working in the round.

Working in Rows

Many flat crochet pieces are worked back and forth in rows, beginning with a chain and foundation row. As you crochet, you alternate from right side to wrong side with each row. At the end of each row, you crochet a turning chain of 1 to 4 stitches, depending on the height of the next row of stitches. If the next row will be single crochet, the turning chain is 1 stitch; half-double crochet: 2 stitches; double crochet: 3 stitches; triple crochet: 4 stitches, etc. The directions will tell you how many chains to make. The turning chain counts as a stitch. For instance, the directions may say, "ch 3 (counts as dc)." At the end of each row, the last stitch is worked into the turning chain from the previous row.

Working in Rounds

Another way to crochet is in rounds, going around in continual circles. When working in the round, the right side of the fabric is always facing you. To begin, the directions will tell you to chain a certain number of stitches and join them into a ring by slip stitching into the beginning chain. For the first round, the stitches are worked into the ring (the hook is inserted into the center of the ring), so the stitches will wrap around the beginning chain (1). When you reach your starting point, slip stitch into the beginning stitch. To continue on the next round, the directions will tell you to crochet a starting chain equal to the height of the stitches in the next round. Then continue, crocheting into the stitches of the previous round, and complete the round by stitching into the starting chain (2).

When working in rounds, it is necessary to note where the round begins and ends to keep track of rows worked. When working in single crochet, the easiest way to mark your rounds is by inserting a different colored piece of yarn in your work, then carrying it up as you work (3). Using a different colored yarn makes it very easy to see and pulls out easily when your work is done.

If you're working in half double crochet, double crochet, or triple crochet, the chain at the beginning of the row creates a seam stitch, so using a marker is not necessary (4). A typical instruction line might read, "ch 3 to begin the round, * work 1 dc in each of the next 2 sts, 2 dcs in next st (inc made), repeat from * around, join with a Sl st to the top of the beg ch 3." This would complete 1 round. The instructions will vary but they always begin with a starting chain and end with a joining at end of the round.

Working in Rounds

Invisible Join/Invisible Fasten Off

When working in the round, connecting the end of the round to the beginning can sometimes seem awkward. Here's a way to connect the last stitch in a way that will leave the connection nearly invisible.

End the last stitch but do not join to the beginning with a slip stitch. Cut the yarn, leaving a tail several inches long. Pull the yarn through the last stitch and set the hook aside. Thread the tail on a tapestry needle, and run the needle under the beginning stitch, pulling the tail through (1). Insert the needle back through the center of the last stitch of the round and pull the tail to the back of the work (not too tightly) (2). This will join the beginning to the end invisibly. Weave the tail into the back of the work.

Invisible Join/Invisible Fasten Off

Slip-Stitch Seam

The slip-stitch join is a favorite of many because it joins pieces easily. Your stitched must be worked loosely to avoid puckering seams. Place right sides together, draw up a loop 1 stitch from the edges of seam, insert hook in next stitch, and draw up a loop; continue in this manner until seam is completed.

Changing Colors

Yarn over in current color, insert hook in next stitch, pull up a loop, drop first color, pull through both loops on hook with new color, leaving a short tail. Cut first color with a short tail. Tie the two tails together in a knot. Weave in ends if necessary. Amigurumi pieces will hide the tails inside the piece.

Magic Ring

With your left hand held sideways, hold yarn vertically across your fingers with the tail end hanging below your pinky. Wrap yarn around the pointer and middle fingers to create an X. Turn your hand to look at the back of your fingers. Insert hook below the right strand of yarn and pick up the left strand. Pull the strand under and up from the right strand. Rotate your hook clockwise about 180 degrees. Chain 1 and drop the yarn off your fingers. Untangle the starting tail from the loop. Holding the tail against the loop, begin working single crochet stitches over both layers (the loop and the tail). Once you've worked the pattern-specified number of stitches, carefully pull the starting tail, which should begin shrinking the loop. Pull the tail until it closes the loop, leaving no hole.

Surface Crochet

This technique works on an already crocheted surface. Instead of working into stitches, you'll work over their surface by inserting your hook below stitches. Insert hook in the "hole" next to a stitch and come out in the "hole" on the other side of the stitch. Yarn over and pull working yarn underneath the stitch. Repeat as many times as the pattern specifies.

Scan to watch a video tutorial on the invisible fasten off.

YARN LIST

Aunt Lydia's Crochet Thread
www.yarnspirations.com/pages/aunt-lydias
Aunt Lydia's Classic Crochet Thread Metallic Size 10
Fairy-Tale Mask, page 69
Small Skeleton Key, page 47

Bernat Yarn
www.bernat-yarn.com
Bernat Blanket Yarn
Dagger, page 58
Large Enemies-to-Lovers Pierced Heart, page 63
Large Magic Mushroom, page 35
Large Poisoned Apple, page 21
Large Skull, page 51
Large Tribute Rose, page 43

Bernat Velvet
Dragon-Eyed Chalice (eye), page 39
Medium Tribute Rose, page 43

Big Twist Yarn
www.bigtwistyarn.com
Big Twist Twinkle
Poison Potion, page 30

Big Twist Value
Fae Ear Cuffs, page 73
Mysterious and Woodland Fae Warriors, page 91

I Love This Yarn
i-love-this-yarn.com
I Love This Yarn Chunky
Faun Beanie, page 77

I Love This Yarn Sport Weight
Book Lover's Bookmark Trio, page 9

I Love This Yarn Worsted Weight
Baby DraGoyle, page 109
Dagger, page 58
Dark Siren (also with I Love This Yarn Metallic), page 83
Fierce Dragon, page 119
Heart-Shaped Love Potion, page 32
Morally Gray Heart Garland/Wall Hanging, page 25
Mysterious and Woodland Fae Warriors, page 91
Small Magic Mushroom, page 35
Small Poisoned Apple, page 21
Small Skull, page 51
Small Tribute Rose, page 43
Small Enemies-to-Lovers Pierced Heart, page 63
Wise Raven, page 99

Lion Brand Pound of Love
lionbrand.com
Lion Brand Pound of Love
Large Skeleton Key, page 47

Loops & Threads
www.michaels.com/shop/yarn-needlework/loops-threads
Loops & Threads Sweet Snuggles
Werewolf Tablet or Book Sleeve, page 15

Yarn Bee
yarn-bee.com
Yarn Bee Cozy Occasion, Yarn Bee Fur the Moment
Werewolf Tablet or Book Sleeve, page 15

Yarn Bee Velvety Smooth
Dragon-Eyed Chalice, page 39

CRAFT YARN COUNCIL STANDARD YARN WEIGHT SYSTEM

Yarn Weight Symbol & Category Names	LACE 0 DENTELLE Liston	SUPER FINE 1 SUPER FIN Super Fino	FINE 2 FIN Fino	LIGHT 3 LÉGER Ligero	MEDIUM 4 MOYEN Medio	BULKY 5 BULKY Abultado	SUPER BULKY 6 TRÉS ÉPAIS Super Abultado	JUMBO 7 GÉANT Jumbo
Type of Yarns in Category	Fingering, 10-count crochet thread	Sock, Fingering, Baby	Sport, Baby	DK, Light Worsted	Worsted, Afghan, Aran	Chunky, Craft, Rug	Super Bulky, Roving	Jumbo, Roving
Crochet Gauge* Ranges in Single Crochet to 4 inches	32–42 double crochets**	21–32 sts	16–20 sts	12–17 sts	11–14 sts	8–11 sts	7–9 sts	6 sts and fewer
Recommended Hook in Metric Size Range	Steel*** 1.6–1.4 mm; Regular hook 2.25 mm	2.25–3.5 mm	3.5–4.5 mm	4.5–5.5 mm	5.5–6.5 mm	6.5–9 mm	9–15 mm	15 mm and larger
Recommended Hook U.S. Size Range	Steel*** 6, 7, 8; Regular hook B–1	B–1 to E–4	E–4 to 7	7 to I–9	I–9 to K–10 ½	K–10½ to M–13	M–13 to Q	Q and larger

** GUIDELINES ONLY: The above reflect the most commonly used gauges and needle or hook sizes for specific yarn categories.*

*** Lace weight yarns are usually knitted or crocheted on larger needles and hooks to create lacy, openwork patterns. Accordingly, a gauge range is difficult to determine. Always follow the gauge stated in your pattern.*

**** Steel crochet hooks are sized differently from regular hooks—the higher the number, the smaller the hook, which is the reverse of regular hook sizing.*

CONTRIBUTORS

CONCEPT CONSULTANT, PATTERN INTRODUCTIONS

Trudi Rae Bartow

CROCHET DESIGNERS

Staci Burns of Fiddlesticks Crochet
fiddlestickscrochet.com
Facebook: FiddlesticksCrochet
Instagram: @fiddlesticks_crochet
Skeleton Keys, page 47
Fairy-Tale Mask, page 69

Lara Carter of Hookedonewe_x
Etsy: Hookedonewexx
Instagram: @hookedonewe_x
TikTok: Hookedonewe_x
Werewolf Tablet or Book Sleeve, page 15

Jodie Chadwick of Handmade By Jodie
Etsy: Jodiesyarn
Facebook: madebyjodiec
Instagram: @handmadebyjodie
TikTok: handmade.by.jodie
Baby DraGoyle, page 109
Fierce Dragon, page 119

Sonia Childers of S.Crochet.Designs
scrochetdesigns.com
Facebook: Sofia.Designs
Instagram: @s.crochet.designs
TikTok: s.crochet.designs
Fae Ear Cuffs, page 73
Faun Beanie, page 77

Daniella Flete of Daniella's Workshop
Etsy: DaniellaWorkshop
Instagram: @daniellasworkshop
Dark Siren, page 83

Mary Penney of Little Brute Creations
Etsy: LittleBruteCreations
Instagram: @littlebrutecreations
Potion Bottles, page 29

Jessica Ryan of Eclectic Jess
eclecticjess.com
Facebook: eclecticjesscrochet
Instagram: @eclectic.jess
TikTok: electicjess
YouTube: @eclecticjess
Morally Gray Heart Garland/Wall Hanging, page 25

CUSTOM CROCHET HOOK DESIGNERS

Blue Dragon courtesy @mollyandmestudio
Gold Dragon courtesy @fiddlesticks_crochet
Laser Sword and **Tower Eye** courtesy @thenerdybirdyartco

ACKNOWLEDGMENTS

I want to give a HUGE thank-you to my husband, Evan, who has been my biggest supporter throughout the process of becoming an author. I was given this opportunity by Quarto from Joy Aquilino during the worst part of my husband's emergency spinal fusion and subsequent surgical drama. He knew the book would be an outlet for me through all the medical stress and it would be a way for me to be present for our two sons (an 8-year-old and autistic 6-year-old) and provide for our home while still being there for his long recovery.

I also want to thank my grandma, who began my love of crochet when I was 16 years old. She gave me one of her favorite blanket patterns and went yarn shopping with me to pick out my colors. Fourteen years later, I've used that spark of inspiration to create a published book!

Thank you to all the authors of novels, specifically those within the romantasy genre, for filling our hearts with the stories that shaped this book. A shout-out to public libraries for being the catalyst of my renewed love of reading! A random spring reading challenge at my local library threw me back into books. If it wasn't for that challenge, I wouldn't be a well-known bookish crocheter, and I may not have been chosen to author this book.

Thank you again to my friends who contributed patterns to this book. I couldn't have done it without you! Lastly, thank you to everyone who has supported me through my social media accounts. I am just your average American girl, but you all have made me feel special. Your support led me to become a social presence large enough to be discovered for this book.

ABOUT THE AUTHOR

A devoted lover of all things nerdy,
Amanda Sennett is a crochet artist and designer
who sells her patterns and handmade plushies on
her Etsy shop and shares her crochet adventures on Instagram,
Facebook, and TikTok. She lives in Northern Michigan.

Instagram: @crochet_by_a_manda_lorian
Facebook: Crochet By A Manda Lorian
TikTok: crochet_by_a_manda_lorian
Etsy: CrochetaMandaLorian / Crochet_By_A_Manda_Lorian

INDEX

This book is dedicated to your inner child, who still looks for the magic in everything and dreams of epic romance. To the adult you, who uses their art to bring that magical adventure to life. To those with a passion for romantic fantasy and all the joy, healing, and love it brings!

Quarto.com

First published in 2025 by Quarry Books, an imprint of The Quarto Group, 100 Cummings Center, Suite 265-D, Beverly, MA 01915, USA.
T (978) 282-9590 F (978) 283-2742

Quarry Books titles are also available at discount for retail, wholesale, promotional, and bulk purchase. For details, contact the Special Sales Manager by email at specialsales@quarto.com or by mail at The Quarto Group, Attn: Special Sales Manager, 100 Cummings Center, Suite 265-D, Beverly, MA 01915, USA.

10 9 8 7 6 5 4 3 2 1

ISBN: 978-0-7603-9673-5

Digital edition published in 2025
eISBN: 978-0-7603-9674-2

Library of Congress Cataloging-in-Publication Data is available.

Concept consultant, project introductions: Trudi Rae Bartow

Contributing crochet designers: Staci Burns, Lara Carter, Jodie Chadwick, Sonia Childers, Daniella Flete, Mary Penney, Jessica Ryan

Many of the stitch instructions in the Crochet Resources (pages 134–139) have been excerpted from *The Complete Photo Guide to Crochet, Second Edition* by Margaret Hubert, published by Creative Publishing international, an imprint of Quarto Publishing Group USA Inc.

Design and page layout: Cindy Samargia Laun
Illustration: Ada Keesler and Adobe Stock / Murhena
Photography: Zack Bowen Photography, except pages 135–139 by CPi, Chris Hubert, Rau + Barber

Printed in China